CABIN

IN THE

CITY

also by John Toren

By the Way
The Seven States of Minnesota
Vacation Days
Mountain Upside Down
The European Dream
Port Wing
All the Things You Are

CABIN

IN THE

CITY

essays

John Toren

NODIN PRESS

A few of these essays originally appeared in *MinnPost, Rain Taxi, Macaroni*, and other regional publications. Special thanks to publisher Norton Stillman, and to the many friends who appear briefly in these pages, like the white flecks in a painting by Corot that bring life and energy to a scene.

9 8 7 6 5 4 3 2 1

ISBN: 978-1-947237-29-2

Library of Congress Control Number: 2021938103

Published by
Nodin Press
5114 Cedar Lake Road,
Minneapolis, MN 55416
www.nodinpress.com

Printed in USA

for Hilary, who shares the adventures

*In earth's variegated dream, a quiet
sustained note sounds, through all other
notes, for those who secretly listen.*

– Friedrich Schlegel

*My working method has more often than
not involved the substraction of weight. I
have tried to remove weight, sometimes from
people, sometimes from heavenly bodies,
sometimes from cities …*

– Italo Calvino

Straight lines shorten distances, and also life.

– Antonio Porchia

Contents

Fall

CABIN

IN THE

CITY

Introduction

This collection takes its title from the introductory essay, in which I describe the woodsy house where my wife, Hilary, and I have lived for more than thirty years. A few of the subsequent essays, which were written sporadically, concern themselves with everyday events at home and the natural surroundings of the place, which sits near a parkland corridor running for several miles on the western edge of Minneapolis: the trees, the passing deer—who enjoy the shrubbery more than we do, and occasionally bed down for the night in the back yard—the sky, the passing seasons, the sounds of the night. And especially the birds. At a time when the pandemic has kept us at home perhaps more than we'd like, it's a pleasure—and a gift—to reflect on such agreeable critters and surroundings.

Then again, more than a few of the essays focus on the "city" rather than the "cabin," recounting forays into town to galleries, shops, parks, and an occasional restaurant, some of which, I'm sorry to report, have by now gone out of business or moved. You'll notice that books also figure prominently in a few of the pieces. I'm not a book hound but I am a reader of sorts, and I've made my living in the book industry for half a century and more. Rereading the collection, I find that the French philosopher Gabriel Marcel and the English essayist

Sir Thomas Browne pop up more often than I can explain, except to say that they write the kind of book I reach for when I'm in a meditative mood.

Social events—family and friends—figure in several essays, as does the preparing and eating of food, especially vegetables, which provide yet one more means of "letting the outside in." You'll come upon a few road trips and a few midsummer parties. I've arranged the pieces by season, so as to avoid the odd juxtaposition of an ice dam and a hollyhock, for example, but they're not strictly chronological.

Call it the good life. It's a hodgepodge of incidental reflections, modest in range, breezy in tone, with no unifying feature, in the end, other than an interest in sharing the poetry that often animates the passing days.

Cabin in the City

I haven't left the house in days, except to shovel the driveway, refill the bird feeder, and deposit the container of vegetable peelings onto the compost pile out back.

During these snowy stretches, when the evening commute becomes treacherous and outstate travel positively reckless, I count my blessings in a) not having a commute at all, and b) feeling no great need to leave town. The other afternoon I was sitting on the couch with a pile of books beside me, watching the sun go down while the fire from a single log roared in the Jøtul stove. We were listening to a brand-new CD of piano music by Sibelius—I might describe it superficially as a cross between Grieg and Saint-Saëns. Hilary had brought home some fresh walleye from the supermarket. And potatoes. When the recital was over we cued it up again.

Yes, there are advantages to having a cabin in the city— that is to say, of having a home in the city that has a woodsy feel. Among other virtues, inhabiting such a dwelling obviates the long drive from the city to a lakeside retreat. It also eliminates the toil and expense of maintaining two domiciles. Of course, the signal purpose of owning a cabin or a "summer place," for many, is to make it possible to exchange, at will, the noise and clutter of city life for the simplicity and quiet of the woods. It follows, therefore, that an urban home must, before all else, be woodsy and quiet to deserve consideration as a "cabin."

I couldn't say when I started using the term "cabin in the city" with reference to our house, but I suspect it was during one of those informal tours people give to guests visiting for the first time. Passing through the conventional living room and the modest kitchen, we would reach the more unusual dining room, a later addition set at a 45-degree angle to the rest of the house with a twelve-foot ceiling and tall windows looking out toward the backyard. Visitors would look out through the windows to the broad deck, the narrow sward of grass below, and the woods beyond.

From that point I would direct their attention to the left, where a new room has just come into view doubling back toward the front of the house. A previous owner—back in the 1950s, I'd guess—converted the breezeway between the house and the garage into a relatively spacious room paneled in knotty pine, with that small Swedish stove I mentioned jutting out into the middle of it. A pair of antique Ojibwe snowshoes now leans against the brick wall behind the stove, and some faded mallard decoys sit on the ledge up top.

"We call this our cabin in the city," I might have said on the occasion of that now-long-forgotten tour.

I was joking, of course.

But over time, the underlying truth of the remark began to sink in. There isn't a lake anywhere nearby, and the woods out back is only twenty feet thick at best; we could probably name the individual trees. But the room has the feel of a cabin, and the house itself, though surrounded on every side by other smallish, one-story, post-war ramblers of similar construction, is only one strip of housing away from an extensive wood running down a steep hill to a marsh, a creek, and a far larger chunk of undeveloped land that continues south for several miles through Theodore Wirth Park and the Minneapolis Chain of Lakes to Minnehaha Creek.

That might explain why deer often pass through the yard and sometimes spend the night, why we hear owls hoot every winter and sometimes find them perched in the yard, why a beautiful fox passes through on odd occasions ... and so on.

This is common suburban stuff, I know, but it keeps us looking out the windows in every season, taking walks around the block, biking down Wirth Parkway to Cedar Lake and beyond, feeding the backyard birds, and listening for the high-pitched keen of the local Cooper's hawk. Light flows into the house at every hour of the day. We often sit in the living room and watch the sun come up, and cook dinner with the pink spread of sunset above the backyard woods just outside the dining room windows.

The first house we owned, in South Minneapolis, didn't have much light. In 1980, the year my mother died, we bought a one-and-a-half story "shotgun" house on Grand Avenue built in 1907. It had crumbling limestone foundations, an octopus furnace, and a coal bin in the basement. (I imagined, way back then, that the coal bin would make a good wine cellar; trouble was, I didn't have any wine.)

The house next door effectively blocked out all light from the south. To the north the view of the neighbor's house—no great thrill—was largely obscured by a massive oak staircase leading up to the second floor. To the east the front porch, with its aluminum screens, allowed little in the way of natural light to enter. Our view to the west was entirely obliterated by the dark oak buffet of the type that had been so popular in 1907, and also during the 1970s, when suburban kids like Hilary and me had returned to the city in search of authenticity and tradition. Let me confess here that I have never stripped an inch of oak in my life, though many of my friends lost precious brain cells liberating their woodwork from the tyranny of paint. All the same, I liked the "mission" look, and still do, up to a point.

The only room in the house that had a view of any kind was a small second-floor room that had a sash window facing west toward a gangly mulberry tree. But the room wasn't big enough to be used for anything except an office, a sewing room, or a nursery. Neither of us spent much time up there.

In contrast, our cabin in the city is filled with light. Looking out, we don't image or dream that we're somewhere else. We're looking at the shapes of the trees, trying to identify the little birds moving through the forest or scraping up the underbrush.

How we happened to arrive here is a story in itself. After spending seven years on Grand Avenue—a major bus route with houses built unusually close to the street—we decided the time had come to start looking for someplace new to live. I say "we" but it was Hilary who initiated the search. She hired a realtor named Pat who showed us quite a number of dwellings in several parts of South Minneapolis—we were still committed city-dwellers—but none of them in our price range were much better than what we already had. In exasperation, she asked if there were any other neighborhoods we'd like to investigate.

At that moment something came to mind. A few years earlier we'd been invited to the birthday party of a friend of a friend, a woman we didn't know well. It was a joint party, however, and it was being held at the other birthday girl's house, in Golden Valley. As we zigged and zagged the final few blocks to that event I remember saying to myself, "Why would anyone live way out here?"

But the house was nice. There were some woods in the back. I even got the impression there was a stream off in the distance, though I couldn't see it.

So when, years later, Pat asked about other neighborhoods, I said, on the basis of that single evening, "Why not line up a few houses in Golden Valley?"

A week later, on a hot summer night, Pat took us around to a succession of smallish ramblers, trim but uniformly undistinguished, all within a few blocks of one other. The last one on the list looked much the same, but when I walked in the door, I noticed that the house extended much farther back than you might have guessed while standing in front of it on the street. As we walked toward the back we entered a room bent at an angle, with tall windows looking out onto a deck. When I saw the two short steps down from the dining room to the den, I had one of those *deja vu* experiences that's both pleasant and creepy. It wasn't just that this house was as nice as the one we'd visited years earlier. It was the same house. Hilary had recognized it the moment we walked in the door. Of course we had to buy it.

When the man we bought it from gave us a house tour, he spent less time discussing the virtues of the plumbing than identifying the various trees he'd planted in the yard. (It might be worth mentioning that he held an executive position in the local Nature Conservancy.) There was a Haralson apple tree and a rare American chestnut in the front yard, and a row of rotund juniper trees formed a privacy screen along the north border in the back, echoing an even more impressive row of blue spruce to the south. The owner and his wife, an environmental lobbyist, had planted a mountain ash, a Russian olive, and a row of gray dogwoods along the edge of the deck. They also maintained a handsome vegetable garden in back, with a pin oak nearby and a buckeye flourishing at the edge of the woods. They'd planted the terraced garden spaces under the bedroom window with wildflowers—wild geraniums, wild honeysuckle, and golden alexander come to mind—and they'd put down trillium, hepatica, and dutchman's breeches in the shadows of the little woods.

The yard is a lot shadier now than it was thirty years ago, and many of the plants I just mentioned are gone, but we've replaced them with other things, and we've also nurtured quite a few of the volunteers that have drifted in over the years.

One obvious drawback to owning a cabin in the city is that you have nowhere to escape to when the rat-race starts getting you down. As readers of these essays will see, Hilary and I often head off for a few days, and sometimes return to the same resort—even the same cabin—year after year. In time, a familiarity and hominess begins to settle in.

I admit, this coziness will never approach the feel of a family cabin with a layered, multigenerational history, but it will also be free of such chores as retrieving the dock that floats away with the ice every spring, removing dead pine needles from the shingles on the roof, and keeping the gas line to the antique propane refrigerator in good repair.

Well, you know what they say: "You can't have everything."

Winter

First Ski—Just Me
and the Squirrels

I was sitting in the living room the other day reading a book about Basque peasants called *In a Hundred Graves* when a cooper's hawk landed on a branch just outside the window.

I think it might have been the most beautiful hawk I've ever seen. I've seen plenty of accipiters in my day; the buffy, wavy, reddish-brown stripes on their chest are often lovely, standing in contrast to the soft blue-gray wing and back feathers. This one had the added virtue of looking relaxed as he perched on the branch, rather than steely-eyed and ever-alert for little songbirds to eat.

Or maybe it was just that *I* was relaxed, and the bird was right outside the window. I was tempted to leap up and run for the camera, which was on top of the piano on the far side of the room, but I would have spooked him, I'm sure. Better just to observe and enjoy.

He changed his position once or twice, fanning his feathers as he did so. Then he flew off, dropping and then rising as he swooped around the corner of the house and out of sight.

That was the start of a beautiful evening. The next episode involved some short-ribs left over from a weekend gathering, a single turnip, some carrots, and a couple of Pillsbury pie crusts, which Hilary and I transformed, with the help of some thyme, nutmeg, onions, and garlic, into one of the best pasties I've ever had.

When I got up this morning it was snowing, but the day was warm, and I decided to go for a morning ski—the first of the season. They've been making snow down at Theodore Wirth Golf Course, a few minutes from the house, for weeks, and also building a big new ski chalet. I happen to like things the way they were—quieter. Then again, I also consider skiing an exercise in woodsy solitude rather than feverish competition.

All the same, we benefit from the man-made snow and the sophisticated grooming techniques that have made Wirth Park perhaps the best skiing destinations in the Cities, and I don't begrudge the park its ever-rising annual skiing fee. Yet I'm afraid the feature that excites me most about all the new construction is the café that's going to be located inside the chalet.

It took me a while to reach the new snow from the parking lot, with the ground all torn up by the construction vehicles and snow-making machines, but I was soon headed out toward the woods on thin but natural snow. The gate at the far end of the par three course was closed, and there was a lock on it, but it wasn't actually locked, so I opened it and went on into the woods.

Beautiful fields, woods, trails. The tracks of a single bicycle. And squirrels everywhere. As the trail looped past Twin Lake and curled back toward the half-built chalet, it occurred to me that the gate at the far end of the loop might also be shut. That's the prettiest section of the trail. The problem is that the gate stands at the bottom of a hill, and if it was shut, I'd have to come to an abrupt stop, or more likely just fall down, to avoid crashing into it.

I prudently walked down the final hill. Yes, the gate was locked. Rather than retracing my path, I crawled under it. It was a tight squeeze. As I was lying on the thin snow, halfway under the gate, I noticed, looking up, how beautiful the trees looked that were arching above my head, each species offering a different silhouette.

I was reminded of my dad, who died a few months ago at the age of ninety-four. I never considered him to be a poetic soul, exactly—he was a chemist by profession—but when we were up in the BWCA together he liked to lie on his back on the ground and take pictures of the trees above his head.

The Old Bell Museum

S ometimes, it's not so bad when a plan falls through.

We'd planned to see an exhibit of Reformation art at the Minneapolis Institute of Arts, but when the day arrived I had trouble securing tickets on the museum website, and we decided to scotch the idea, at least for the time being.

An empty Saturday yawned in front of us.

Our first stop was to the Bell Museum of Natural History—the old Bell. It was scheduled to close permanently in a few weeks, though at that time funding for a proposed new building on the Saint Paul Campus remained problematic. Being on campus again evoked a few memories of student life, mostly pleasant: hanging out with friends, working part-only time, reading books, almost at random.

As we approached the Bell Museum, we requested the senior rate at the front desk in the lobby, and then I said, "I used to take little kids on tours through this place. Is that good for an additional discount?"

The two women behind the counter were barely out of their teens. "We get quite a few former tour guides through here," one of them said, smiling graciously. "Maybe we'll come up with something soon."

"Well, it would be pretty hard to verify," I said. "Anyway, we're happy to chip in."

By a stroke of luck, the Minnesota Ornithological Union was holding its annual "paper session" that morning. We're not members of that organization, but the man standing at the door to the auditorium said, "Go on in and listen to a few of the presentations. If you find it worthwhile, you can pay on your way out." He handed me a schedule:

– Tracking Movement Patterns of Common Terns
– Wastewater Pond Birding Access Initiative
– Owls to Orchids: Magic and Mystery in Northern Bogs
– Insights into the Evolution of Red-winged Blackbirds
– Citizen Science in the Digital Age
– Kirkland's Warbler Population in the Upper Midwest

A session had just concluded, so we stepped inside the auditorium, and I was reminded that I had listened here to the last lectures given by the anthropologist E. Adamson Hoebel before his retirement. For many years that hallowed space was also the venue for the University Film Society, where I first saw *Jules and Jim, Pierrot le Fou, Chimes at Midnight, Tree of the Wooden Clogs, L'Avventura*, and many other classics in an era when a theater screening was the only way you *could* see a rare or European film.

A few of the conference attendees were exiting, but many were chatting in small groups, and I got the impression that most of the seats were already spoken for, so we went upstairs to take a look at the dioramas. The halls there were also clogged with birders chatting in twos and threes at booths that had been set up by local outdoor organizations. Among them we spotted an old family friend, Chet Meyers, standing behind a table for a society dedicated to rehabilitating habitat for the red-headed woodpecker.

"We saw a red-headed woodpecker on the Blue Hills Trail at Sherburne last summer," I said.

"We've been working to get a nesting pair up there," he said, "and there's also one on the Mahnomen Trail."

The woman behind the nearby table for the Eloise Butler Wildflower Garden urged me to take one of their newsletters. I declined, telling her that I was already familiar with it, because I had designed it. That remark, coming out of left field, didn't quite sink in, but little matter. We were soon discussing great horned owls, acorn flour, and buckthorn removal like old friends.

At the Sax-Zim Bog display I asked the man behind the table what he thought of the Trailside Restaurant in Meadowlands.

"It's OK, " he replied, "but I usually go to Wilbert's over in Cotton."

Then I said, "I've never seen a boreal chickadee. Do you have any ideas about where I might get lucky?"

"Sure," he said. He grabbed a map of the bog, which extends over many square miles, and proceeded to mark three places that could hardly miss.

The booths were interesting and informative, but the dioramas were better—the wolves, the bear, the caribou, but also the smaller displays with martin and fisher, rough-legged hawk, woodcock, lynx. I looked lovingly at the marshland exhibits, though they had bored me forty years ago, largely because at the time all the shorebirds looked alike to me. And I looked with equal fondness at the landscapes of the other dioramas—Inspiration Peak, Shovel Point, Gunflint Beach—not only because they were beautiful, but because I now recognized many of them, having visited the landscapes they depict.

Then it was off to the St. Paul campus of the university, with two stops in between: first at Potter's Pasties, which occupies a truly bohemian space in the basement of a convenience store on East Como Avenue, and then at the Sisu cross-country ski and sauna shop on Eustis Street, to look at the backcountry skis.

As we approached the Ag campus we happened to pass the site of the new Bell Museum, which was still under construction at the time, but already stunning. Our destination was the Goldstein Gallery, tucked away on the third floor of McNeal Hall. A forty-year design retrospective was scheduled to open at 1:30, but at 1:45 the gallery was still dark, and we made our way back to the car. The sun had come out, and suddenly it didn't seem like such a big deal to hightail it down to the Barnes and Noble in Galleria, at the opposite end of town, to hear Michael Chabon read.

* * *

The new Bell Museum opened in the summer of 2018 to widespread acclaim. And nostalgia aside, it's hard to deny that it's a better facility in many ways than the old one. The best parts of the old Bell—the dioramas—were disassembled, cleaned, and brought along to the new building at great expense, where they were placed in spaces even more congenial to them than their old settings. The halls of the old Bell were brightly lit and echoed the voices of school groups all too well. The new Bell consists of spaces rather than halls. They're dimly lit, and large murals of trees hang from the rafters, which gives the dioramas a warm, outdoorsy feel while also helping them shine all the more. These spaces also contain plenty of Plexiglas kiosks focusing on mussels, plant communities, mushrooms, individual bird and mammal species, and more abstract ecological concepts. Everywhere you turn, there's something new to learn.

In the midst of all the talent and taste that went into this urban masterpiece, only one detail struck me as odd: A huge concrete sundial sits right in the middle of the parking lot, taking up at least eight parking spaces. Meanwhile, the lot is often full, and eager visitors are directed to an overflow lot three blocks away.

The Barrow's Goldeneye

A warm January is nice. But a gray and dreary day calls for some sort of response. Ours was to head for the Mississippi River north of town to see about locating a Barrow's Goldeneye that had been reported in the vicinity of Anoka by three or four birders.

The common goldeneye is often seen in these parts, even in the wintertime, presuming there's some open water. It's a beautiful duck, and full of character, a frisky diver, more compact than most ducks, with a somewhat elongated forehead and short bill that gives its head an interesting shape.

The Barrow's goldeneye looks just the same—except that the white spot on its cheek looks like a comma rather than a circle, and the pattern of markings on its back is different.

Goldeneyes tend to travel in flocks—up and down the Mississippi River, for example, usually on the opposite side from the one you're on. We reached the river in Champlin, a twenty-minute drive north, and pulled into the riverside park. I was trying to get the spotting scope rigged up when a pick-up came to a stop nearby.

"Any luck?" the man said.

"You mean the Barrow's goldeneye? We just got here."

"I saw it earlier this morning. Haven't seen it lately. A lot of the goldeneyes are across the river in front of that house—can you see it?—with the big front porch."

It was a long ways away.

A man with a very large camera was sitting on a stool near the beach, poised and ready.

"See anything?" I asked, walking over his way.

"No. But maybe you can get those goldeneye to cross the river and pose right here in front of the beach."

"Sure. If you'll email me the photo. Did you know there's a rare one out there?"

"I had no idea."

We decided to cross the river ourselves to check out another large flock that was milling about just offshore in front of Peninsula Park in Anoka, barely visible from where we were standing. On our way out of Champlin I made what may have been the best sighting of the day—the sign above the storefront of Q Fanatic BBQ.

"That place often shows up in the top ten lists," I said. "We should come back for lunch."

Five minutes later we were lined up along with three other birders on the east bank of the Mississippi, looking through the trees at a large raft of goldeneyes.

"You see anything?" I said.

"I've got the Barrows right in my scope. Trouble is, he only comes up for a second or two and then dives again. Oh, he's up again…Now he's down."

The man directed me to the part of the raft where the Barrow's was diving. "Look through that V in the trees, just beyond the ice flow." I didn't see him.

"He's up! Now he's down."

I think the three other birders must have seen him, but we didn't. I started to rationalize: *three knowledgeable birders attest to the presence of a Barrow's goldeneye within that raft of ducks. I see the raft of ducks. So it might be said that I have seen a Barrow's goldeneye, though I have no idea which duck it was.* That would not have been a very satisfying "sighting."

I don't mind asking questions; it's obvious that we're not experts. "So, do you look for the facial markings or the coloration on the back?"

"Look for the darker back. It's very distinctive. You'll never see that hook in the white spot. Oh. Now he's up again! ... Now he's down. Here. Take a look through my scope."

I didn't see it.

A few minutes later we walked up a rise along the mushy sidewalk to a spot where two other birders were standing. One was the man we'd talked to across the river in Champlin.

"He's out there," the man said.

The view was better here. The man tried to describe where the Barrows was situated in the flock. Then I saw it. The obvious comma-shaped white marking in front of the eye. The bird had grown tired of diving, evidently, and was taking it easy. Nice.

Hilary took a long look and also saw the variation on the back. I looked away, then saw it again. When two other birders with their scopes came over, I (suddenly the expert) tried to help them locate the position between the trees and in the midst of a grouping of perhaps eighty other almost identical birds that were drifting slowly downstream in the midst of large chunks of floating ice.

Having driven this far, we decided to continue up the river a few miles to Monticello, where hundreds of trumpeter swans congregate every winter. There weren't any swans in sight when we got there, just a few hundred mallards. The swans had taken advantage of the melting snow to head out into the nearby cornfields to feed. But Jim Lawrence, who lives next door to the overlook, happened to be standing there. His wife used to feed the birds and he promised her he'd continue the practice when she died. He showed us a panorama on his iPhone of a recent day (or perhaps it was a year ago) when more than 1,600 swans were present.

Jim told us the story of how the swans, once considered extinct in North America, had made such a comeback locally, and he also shared quite a bit of information about his free lance coyote hunting in nearby Sherburne National Wildlife Refuge at the request of the local rangers.

We decided to take backroads along the river back to Champlin rather than return to the freeway, and this took us through a village I'd never visited before—Dayton. Not much going on there, by the look of things. But sometimes you'd be surprised.

We capped off our gray winter field trip with some heat— at the Q Fanatic BBQ. Lots of meat on those ribs, and the beans and slaw were also tasty.

I later read a review of the unprepossessing place in *The Heavy Table* that began as follows:

> *It is infuriating that Q Fanatic is one of Minnesota's best-kept gastronomic secrets. This is a place that should be elbow-to-elbow crowded, seven nights a week, and resisting the temptation to expand and choke on its own success. Q Fanatic is doing barbecue at a level that stacks up, rib for rib, against the kind of stuff they're doing at the grand-champion 17th Street Bar & Grill near East St. Louis, or at Allen and Son in Chapel Hill, NC. This is stuff that kicks Famous Dave's into the dust and merits the long drive from*

the metro area. Grit your teeth, and get in the car. There is a rainbow of perfectly cooked meat waiting at the end of your voyage.

If ribs alone don't make it worth a trip, you can always stop along the river and try to hunt up a Barrow's goldeneye.

Pea Soup

A hedge fund manager made headlines the other day for paying 285 million—or was in 385 million?—for a half-finished apartment in Manhattan. But on a gray, slightly snowy day in January, it's hard to beat sitting in an overstuffed chair in front of the fire in a suburban rambler with a mug of split-pea soup in one hand and a copy of Montaigne's *Essays* in the other.

The snow is so light you can shovel it with one arm, though it's easier with two. And birds seem to be arriving at the feeder from all over the neighborhood: pileated, red-breasted, and downy woodpeckers; five or six cardinals at a time, shifting places or waiting their turn on the naked branches of the Amur maple trees near the fence. There's a frenzy in the air, and it's exciting to witness.

I made the pea soup yesterday, and it taught me two lessons. The first is that green pea soup can be just as good as yellow pea soup. I'd been hung up on the French-Canadian yellow pea variety, but I couldn't find yellow peas at the grocery store. Also, in boiling up the green split peas, I noticed for the first time that they actually smell like fresh green peas. It's a nice, summer-time smell.

You may not be aware that Minnesota is the nation's largest producer of green peas. Farmers here plant ninety thousand acres a year, and the revenue they generate from this activity averages $38 million annually. This means that if all the pea farmers in Minnesota pooled their proceeds for ten years, they, too, could buy a half-finished penthouse in Manhattan. Maybe they could set up a time-share.

The second thing I learned is that it's a good idea to over-load your pea soup with sautéed onions, celery, and carrots. Don't hold back. (What else are you going to do with that celery, anyway?) Summer savory is the preferred herb (especially in Quebec), but go easy on the salt, because that big chunk of salt pork is going to have a profound effect on the flavor.

At a certain point in the afternoon, it's a good idea to go out and get some air. Hilary and I drove down to the Lake Harriet Kite Festival, and we even brought along a kite I'd gotten recently as a birthday gift. In the end, we left the kite in the car, but it was fun to be out wandering on the ice with several hundred other winter enthusiasts.

The display of airborne kites was not overwhelming—a few little dots of color here and there against the gray sky. Not only was the wind feeble, but the ice was covered with a thin veneer of loose snow, which made it difficult for kite-fliers to run across the frozen lake at any great speed without taking a fall.

An ice fishing contest had been organized for the kids, several food trucks were parked in the lot near the bandshell, and volunteers were dispensing free coffee to anyone who would make a contribution to the Art Shanty Villages, which lost out on their grant and will not be in operation this winter.

Just being out on the open expanse of a frozen lake, with people passing this way and that in random directions like a scene from *Dr. Zhivago,* is a thrill. At one booth they were renting fat-tire bikes, and we could see little squadrons of cyclists pedaling across the ice in the distance.

All the way there and back on Wirth Parkway we listened to a mysterious CD called *Praying* that was recorded in a Norwegian church by the Karl Ivar Refseth Trio. We're talking here about a vibraphone, a double bass, and an alto saxophone, or occasionally a duduk—an ancient double reed wind instrument from Armenia made of apricot wood.

Back home, I faced a challenge that no hedge fund manager will ever face. The fire had gone out while we were gone, but it was still smoldering. Some golden pieces of split cedar kindling were lying in a wicker basket on the hearth. I had split them myself from the butt end of a long cedar beam I'd been cherishing in the garage for years. I knew that if I tossed one or two of those pieces in, they would soon burst into flame and revive the fire. They would smell heavenly, burn perfectly, and crackle like nobody's business. So beautiful and so precious. But supplies are limited.

The Luminary Loppet

The Loppet festival takes place every winter at Theodore Wirth Park—depending on the snow cover and the weather. The events include several high-class cross-country ski races, a dogsled race, some skijoering, and a fat tire bike race across the frozen lakes of Minneapolis.

This year the snow wasn't good, which made it impossible to ski the traditional course that starts at the chalet and ends up at Lake Calhoun. But they'd been making snow in the park all winter, which made it possible to run several of the long races as multi-lap loops within the park.

The park is just down the hill from our house, and I walked down to see the Hoigaard's marathon on Saturday morning. It was quite a scene. Someone was grilling sausages on the terrace of the chalet, and the smell of grease and smoke in the winter air reminded me of Boy Scout camp. A pleasant reminder. There were waxing stations for the contestants, and REI was giving away metal drinking cups at a booth. Skiers were whizzing past out on the course and also wandering here and there in their form-fitting outfits. The excited hubbub, the bright colors of the tight-fitting clothes, the unnatural posturing, and all the dogs reminded me of some paintings I saw years ago on the walls of the Palazzo Schifanoia ("escape from boredom") in Ferrara.

I stood behind the fence at a tricky downhill turn for a while. The two men standing next to me seemed to know quite a few of the skiers. When I heard them talking about a guy named "Toren" I was tempted to butt into the conversation. It might have been a long lost relation from Sweden! I later found out that one of the racers was four-time U.S. Olympian Torin Koos. He won the sprints that day but was aced out of the marathon championship by a local skier.

Later in the day we went down with some friends to ski the Luminary Loppet, a non-competitive shuffle around Lake of the Isles that's made more interesting by the presence of hundreds of luminaria—candles protected by ice enclosures in various shapes and sizes, some of them ten feet high. The chief thrill of this event is being out after dark, wandering the lake past innumerable candles in the midst of hundreds of people all of whom are wearing their entry ticket around their neck—a plastic tube that glows in the dark in green or yellow or red. The organizers have punctuated the trek with points of interest including the Ice Cropolis, Ice Henge, fire dancers, and Ice-ter Island. Fires are blazing at most of these featured stops. Some serve cocoa, others are distributing free Kind Bars.

No doubt for many of the adults, the Surly Beer Tent is a highlight. You get a free beer and a salted nut roll, though it seems to me the high-decibel hip-hop band was more than a little out of place. How about a Finnish accordion or two?

Due to the miserable snow-cover, the event organizers dropped the idea of skiing the loop and instructed everyone to walk. That was definitely a good idea, though I talked to one woman who was doing the entire loop with her kids, on skates.

Northwoods Journal

It was dusk when we pulled into the Mont Royal super-market—a place where the lighting director probably makes more than the produce buyer. It was a glitzy shopping experience of the kind I don't generally associate with Duluth. We'd come looking for fresh fish and bought a pound and a half of lake trout. The butcher was excited to sell it to us. "Caught just yesterday in Bayfield," he said enthusiastically. Everyone else seemed to be buying frozen shrimp and scallops for their New Year's Eve party.

It was dark by the time we got to Two Harbors. Not a big deal, though it seemed odd to arrive at our cabin in Castle Danger without having gotten a single good look at the big lake. We could hear it, however. It was roaring. We breaded, fried, and ate the fish, took a walk in the dark along the approach road to the resort, then built a fire in the glassed-in fireplace. Now I'm poking my nose into a collection of essays by Martin Heidegger—why not? He's trying to convince me, based on the etymology of the German word, that "building" is the same thing as "dwelling." Think about it. It's a ridiculous argument, though it highlights Heidegger's singular preference for passive rather than active notions.

Tomorrow we'll ski.

* * *

Morning. Two red-breasted mergansers (I think) just drifted by outside the window.

* * *

We skied Gooseberry Falls State Park. Plenty of snow cover. Two hours without seeing a soul. These are our favorite North Shore trails. The woods are varied and generally open, never flat but seldom treacherous. We climb gently, pausing to look down at the gorge of the Gooseberry River from the bridge, rising further to a log shelter from which point you can look north across miles of largely uninhabited woods—a mottled pattern of frosty grays and rich pine greens stretching to the horizon. The rest of the loop is mostly downhill. We took our usual route but tacked on another small loop at the base of the "deer yard" that took us up a little hill to another bivouac shelter with views to the south.

Later, on our way out of the parking lot, we came upon four pine grosbeaks pecking at the salt on the road.

* * *

After lunch we headed back out to ski the municipal trails in Silver Bay. It was something of a shock to arrive at the parking lot and find it almost full.

The trails here are narrow. They run through the dark spruce woods maybe thirty feet up the bank from the Beaver River. The afternoon sun coming across the frozen river penetrated the vegetation here and there to give the woods a genuine sparkle. A half-mile in, the trail leaves the river and the countryside becomes more open, occasionally meadow-like, which makes it easier to see the spectacular rock outcroppings in the distance to the north, hundreds of feet high.

On our way back we took a detour along County 4 to Lax Lake, where the multicolored ice-fishing shacks can be beautiful, set against the same rugged hills we were skiing below. There weren't all that many houses out on the ice—too early in the winter?—but little matter; few things are more brilliant than to be out on a snow-covered lake in full glare of winter sun.

* * *

I was cooking up a lamb stew with white beans and vegetables when Hilary got back from testing out a new set of aluminum snowshoes we'd inherited. "I haven't quite mastered the snowshoes," she said, "but the moon is spectacular."

I went outside to take a look. There was a crescent moon, more golden than usual. There was Venus, above and to the left, and then Mars, higher up, smaller.

* * *

Having read a few more pages of Heidegger's essays I arrive at the conclusion that Being isn't all that interesting. Can anything be done about Being? I think not. Let's put it aside, therefore, and redirect our attention toward a more important concept: Value.

So I turn to Kenneth Rexroth's *One Hundred Poems from the Chinese*, where I read:

> *Men, in moments of*
> *Idleness, occupy their minds*
> *with the vacuity of*
> *Feminine eyebrows...*
> —Ou Yang Hsiu

The poet must have had a rough life, for he goes on to say:

> *—who ever*
> *has been benefitted by the*
> *presence of a woman? Still,*
> *my lewd heart yearns for the past …*

* * *

Turning to the French thinker Gabriel Marcel, I read:

> *Might it not be said that to create is always to create above*
> *oneself? And is it not exactly, also, in this sort of connection*
> *that the word "above" assumes its specific value?*

A little further on I come upon a remark that might well have been aimed, in the kindest way possible, at Marcel's German colleague Heidegger:

> *When he coins a new word, a philosopher is often the vic-*
> *tim of an illusion. The strange and surprising impression*
> *produced on him by his new word often prevents him from*
> *seeing that there is nothing strange or surprising about the*
> *thought it expresses.*

* * *

And so, we step outside again to view the stars. A clear night, constellations everywhere, the moon still twenty degrees above the horizon.

And then a bonus—a pack of coyotes, not that far away, start yipping like mad.

Cozy North

It's been a great winter, snowy and cold like they were in the 1960s, when I walked a mile to school every day through the bitter morning air down the backstreets of Mahtomedi.

Our snow blower has been on the blink for several years now, and just this morning, as I chucked piles of snow up the bank on either side of the driveway, I stopped often to admire the peaceful atmosphere and the beautiful sunlight suffusing the neighborhood at dawn, the air totally free of the smell of gasoline.

I learned this year, entirely by chance, how nice it can be to have a very light shovel. Hilary's parents gave us theirs when they moved into a senior apartment: a square sheet of corrugated red plastic stapled to a wooden dowel. It looked like a cheap toy, and we took it merely to get it out of their way. For years I've been using a thick metal plow-like shovel that's great for scraping across the concrete driveway but weighs about twenty pounds. The first time I lifted snow with the new "toy" I was amazed.

Settling myself here in front of the computer, I see my neighbor Alice shoveling the heaps of snow that the snow-plows left at the end of her driveway this morning. I ought to go out and help her, but I've got a crick in my back, and as she says herself, with a bittersweet grin, "I've got two lazy teenage girls sleeping the day away inside."

Brendan, my neighbor across the street, has a snow-blower the size of a Zamboni, and he sometimes helps her out. But now I see his wife, Sara, out on their driveway with a shovel, and I'm reminded that his machine is on the fritz, and he, too, has got a crick in his back.

It's a bright morning, made brighter by the pristine snow. No summer day could rival this luminosity. And to top things off, the perfect light penetrates far deeper into the house than it does in summer when the sun is higher in the sky.

I call it February Light—not an imaginative name, I realize, but it's accurate, and naming something reminds you, year after year, that it exists.

* * *

Speaking of naming things, in the run-up to the Superbowl, which Minneapolis hosted in 2018, attempts were made to "rebrand" Minnesota as a wonderland separate from, and presumably more distinctive than, Iowa, Wisconsin, the Dakotas, and the Upper Midwest at large. The effort was a harmless one, though it harbored commercial overtones that few Minnesotans—modest to a fault—could get excited about. "Bold North," for example, was largely a flop, absurd and self-defeating. After all, the Viking marauders of yore didn't go around exclaiming, "Watch out; we're BOLD!" They just appeared unexpectedly in their supple longboats, growled unintelligibly, chopped off a few heads, took the monastery gold and jewels, and continued on their way.

In any case, to be useful, a regional moniker ought to refer to a region, rather than a single state. Minnesota finds itself in the pleasant but unusual situation of being of the border of three regions: the Great Plains, the boreal forest (aka the North Woods), and the eastern hardwoods. Its proximity to Lake Superior gives it an added touch of romance, but its only claim to unique northerliness lies in the Northwest Angle, a curious anomaly accessible only from Canada that juts a few miles north of the 49th parallel.

Even this claim has been challenged by Alaskan journalists, who harbor the strange notion that Alaska is part of the United States. I found the column of Craig Medred, "Geographical Thievery," especially nimble and amusing. He would have no way of knowing, I guess, that to most Americans, Alaska is simply Alaska: outsized, empty, cold, wild, wonderful, and (thanks to Sarah Palin and friends) weird. No other state or region can compare or compete with it, and everyone knows that. It isn't in the contest.

Yet we ought to admit that Minnesotans are grasping at straws when they take pride in having the only indigenous wolf packs (in the lower 48), half of all the peat bogs (in the lower 48), the coldest recorded temperatures (in the lower 48), and the most visited wilderness area in the U.S. These features are all found in the largely uninhabited northern tier of the state, and they're basically fortuitous spill-overs from Canada. Inhabitants of Albert Lea and Willmar probably don't much care about such things.

In any case, it seems to me that Bold North has a false ring that makes it even worse than the slogan that emerged from the 1991 World Series: We Like It Here. Nowadays that isolationist stance won't do. The Twin Cities isn't growing as fast as Denver or Seattle, and city fathers are worried.

Most Minnesotans aren't worried about such things—quite the reverse—and we're slightly embarrassed by all the manufactured hoopla. Therefore, in place of Bold North, let me suggest an alternative: Cozy North—ice dams on the roof, fire in the fireplace, woodpeckers at the suet feeder, pasty in the oven, accordion music on the stereo. (Well, let's not get carried away!) February light streaming in, book in hand (maybe Will Weaver's *The Last Deer Hunter*).

Bold North stubbed its toe with the Vikings; Cozy North took us all the way to the top at the winter Olympics in Pyeonchang, South Korea, with the Chisholm Curling Club Team.

A SURVEY BY THE Pew foundation revealed recently that the city of Minneapolis, which ranks near the top of the list as far as education, health, culture, and aquatic resources are concerned, lies somewhere very close to the bottom among cities that people actually want to move to. Denver led the survey's list of popular cities to relocate in, followed by San Diego and Seattle, with other southern and western cities close behind. Among major cities, Minneapolis was surpassed only by Kansas City, Cincinnati, Cleveland, and Detroit in its lack of appeal.

When I read such things, questions immediately spring to mind—questions the researchers probably didn't think to ask. In particular, I would like to know how many of the people who want to live in Denver or Seattle have spent much time there. I think it would also be worth finding out what percentage of the people who live in such high-ranking cities as San Antonio, Tampa, and Phoenix, actually want to *stay* there. Perhaps they, too, are longing to live somewhere else.

I suspect that most Minneapolitans would be pleased to learn that only 16% of Americans would consider moving here. And we all know why—it's too cold! With few exceptions, only natives and long-time residents have the wherewithall to reap the full fruits of the Minnesota experience.

Let me give you an example. Each year at about this time, I'm startled once again by the beauty of February Light. I've mentioned it before. The sun has been rising in the sky and it's getting brighter, but it still flows deeply into the house from its relatively low position. The snow has been on the ground for a while, and even though we haven't had much of a thaw yet this year, the sun's radiant heat has been enough to melt the surface sufficiently to create tiny crystals that reflect the light like a carpet of diamond-dust. The cold air doesn't hold much moisture, but when the temperature rises to twenty degrees or so, it begins to give off a moist, balmy fragrance. Add to all this the visual onslaught of a brilliant blue sky and the roaring sound of the gusty wind making its way through the spruce branches, and you've got an experience that people in Los Angeles or Tucson can only dream about.

Ivory Gull – I Should Care

Nature is mysterious. Among the more intriguing of the inexplicable phenomena it throws in our path is the movement of birds. Bird migration is not well understood, and it's even more difficult to explain why birds occasionally diverge widely from their common range. But it certainly adds to the fun.

Duluth is a year-round hot-spot for unexpected arrivals from the north. Unusual sightings from my early birding days include the sight of a wimbrel wandering in a field at a resort near Castle Danger and a parasitic jaeger harassing gulls just offshore out on Park Point.

In the last few days many visitors to Canal Park have spotted an extremely rare visitor from the Arctic: an ivory gull. I had heard about the sightings, and I knew we were heading to the North Shore for our annual new year's ski, but I didn't put two and two together until we were half way to Duluth. Hilary was reading an article about the bird to me from the *Star-Tribune*.

"We could go out and see if it's still there … after we pick up some sandwiches at the smoked fish shop." Of course we could!

It wasn't hard to find the bird. We pulled into the parking lot next to the marine museum and wandered over to the small clutch of people fiddling with their spotting scopes.

No one seemed very excited. It was as if they were tending their children at a neighborhood park, but not paying much attention.

Two of the men were discussing lenses. Finally one of them turned to me and said, "The ivory gull is over there, on the far side of the canal. And right here, on the second lamp-post down, you can see a black-backed gull."

The ivory gull was easy to see through binoculars. It was standing all alone, mostly white, but with black blotches on the face and a few black dots on the wings.

This little bird rarely strays from Arctic ice flows, where it feeds on fish and the remains of Inuit sea mammal kills; it has been known to harass injured polar bears.

What was it doing in Duluth?

Strange as it may sound, a mangled specimen of the same species was found a few days earlier on Conner's Point in Superior, just across the harbor. Perhaps it had been attacked by the rare gyrfalcon that's been spotted repeatedly in recent days, hanging out amid the nearby grain elevators. Who knows? In any case, I found it nice to imagine that two young gulls decided to take an exploratory trip to more moderate climes, rather than that a single immature gull had gotten disoriented and later found itself a long way from home.

Taking another long look at the gull, I saw traces of neither sorrow nor confusion on its face. It just looked like a little white gull bearing an inscrutable gull-like expression.

I turned my atention to an ore boat approaching the canal through the light fog.

"I'm not a birder," one of the men in the little group said. "I'm a boat-watcher. I have 2,300 images on my website." He repeated the url but it was long and I didn't catch it.

"That boat is a mile and a half out."

"What's it doing on the lake at this time of year?" I said.

"It's a Canadian ship. It's coming into port to refuel," he surprised me by saying. "Then it will head up to Two Harbors to load with ore."

He didn't mention where it would be taking the ore, but as the vessel passed through the narrow canal I took a few pictures, and later I looked it up.

The *Michipicoten* (formerly the *Elton Hoyt II*) has an interesting history. It was built in 1952 and towed up the Mississippi and Illinois Rivers to Lake Michigan. Thus it isn't as large as many of the lakers, and was less often used over the years. But it was eventually retrofitted with a diesel engine and automatic unloaders, and its smaller size made it possible for her to visit some of the lesser ports on the Great Lakes.

In 2003, Lower Lakes Towing, a Canadian shipping company, bought the vessel and renamed it the *Michipicoten*, in honor of the river near where the ship often sails.

I had never heard of the Michipicoten River, so I looked it up. It flows into Lake Superior north of Sault Ste. Marie near the metropolis of Wawa, Ontario. Other ships in the little fleet, including the *Cuyahoga*, the *Saginaw*, and the *Mississagi*, also have local connections.

As the ship entered the canal, someone on the lift bridge let go a blast on the horn, and the *Michipicoten* responded with several of its own. All the birders had come over to the canal to watch it go by. Some people waved at members of the crew who were scurrying along the side-decks.

It's a majestic sight, watching such a large vessel make the turn toward Superior Harbor, framed by the lift-bridge. But before it had vanished from view we all headed back to the parking lot. The ivory gull seemed to have flown off. In any case, everyone had gotten a good look at it.

For most of us, the allure of sighting a rare bird fades pretty fast, but one avid birder, Jim Williams, who often writes for the newspapers, spent five hours with the bird during which time it only vocalized once.

We were happy to sit in the car eating spicy Sitka Sushi sandwiches from the Northern Waters Smokehaus, made from wild Alaskan sockeye gravlax, with cucumber, shredded veggies, pickled ginger, cilantro, chili sauce, and wasabi mayonnaise, all stuffed into a hero roll.

I get the same thing every time we visit.

Meet My New Friend

L ife is peppered with serendipitous meetings, which sometimes prove long-lasting and rewarding. I believe I had one just the other day. On the basis of some passing reference that I no longer remember, I requested three books from the library (this is the boring part; bear with me):

Essays on Kant and Hume, by Lewis White Beck
David Hume: Philosophical Historian
The Essays of Hume

They all came in on the same day, and having nothing better to do, I drove over to the library to pick them up.

The first was a disappointment. I expected to receive a volume by a world-class expert explicating in detail how Hume was right and Kant was wrong about almost everything. It became obvious immediately that Beck was a Kant enthusiast.

The second was much better. It explores the fact, using the Scottish master's own texts, that although Hume (rightly) debunked the concept of causality, he went on to write a six-volume history of England in which events follow one another in seemingly causal fashion. Recognizing that this was a dense but valuable piece of scholarship, not to be absorbed in an afternoon, I ordered a hardcover copy online--as it happens, the only one currently available in the United States.

But the real surprise was the third volume. I had requested the essays of David Hume, but what I received was the essays of Leigh Hunt! Strange. The call number was correct: 824.0 H94. This volume, published in 1905, was mis-cataloged from the start, and had been sitting on the shelf with the wrong title and the wrong author for more than a century!

The book still had a card in the front pocket. Someone had checked it out on March 18, 1948, and was probably as surprised as I was when he or she took a look at it.

My first thought was to toss it in the return bin on my way out to the car. But that would have been an insult to the workers who had gone to the trouble of retrieving it from the Minitex off-site Access Center downtown, placed it into a gray plastic tub, loaded it onto a truck, and shipped it off to Golden Valley, where another low-paid worker had rolled it out on a metal cart and shelved it in precisely the slot appropriate to the number on my library card.

I had *heard* of Leigh Hunt, of course. If you'd asked me, I would have placed him vaguely in the third tier of English essayists of the Romantic era, below Thomas de Quincy (second tier) and also Charles Lamb and William Hazlitt (first tier). But I'd never actually *read* him. Well, here was my chance.

The first essay in the book was devoted to the geranium sitting on Hunt's window sill. Seven pages on that subject. I liked it. Even on the first page Hunt hits upon one of the cardinal virtues of the geranium: the smell of its leaves (similar to that of a tomato plant) which remain on your fingers after you've touched it.

But Hunt hasn't touched it. He's only *thinking* about touching it:

We perceive, in imagination, the scent of those good-natured leaves, which allow you to carry off their perfume on your fingers; for good-natured they are, in that respect above almost all plants, and fittest for the hospitalities of your rooms. The very feel of the leaf has a household warmth in it something analogous to clothing and comfort.

As I read further, this was the tone I encountered throughout: accurate descriptions by a sensitive observer who has moved beyond the "knowing" irony and cynicism of sophisticated commentators to present us with experience in its freshness and innocence.

Emboldened, I committed myself to a travel piece of thirty-two pages located a little deeper in the collection called "A Walk from Dulwich to Brockham." I don't know where either of these municipalities are, though I believe Hunt was traversing, on foot, a stretch of countryside southeast of London proper that might, today, be referred to as the North Downs.

This essay intrigued me because I have myself written longish essays about places no one has been to, with digressions at every step of the way about flora and fauna, architecture, history, and chance meetings with the locals. I have always wondered whether such things can really hold the interest of someone who hasn't been there. Well, Hunt's piece held mine.

On the one hand, his descriptions are peppered with philosophical asides, for example: "Remoteness is not how far you go in point of ground, but how far you feel yourself from your commonplaces." He praises out-of-the-way country museums:

In going to see the pictures in a beautiful country village, people get out of their town common-places, and are better prepared for the perception of other beauties, and of the nature that makes them all."

On the ecclesiastical architecture of the day: "A barn is a more classical building than a church with a fantastical steeple to it."

Passing a field of poppies:

Poppies, with their dark ruby cups and crowned heads, the more than wine color of their sleepy silk, and the funeral look of their anthers, seem to have a meaning about them beyond other flowers. They look as if they held a mystery at their hearts, like sleeping kings of Lethe.

Hunt is convinced, as are many experts today, that walking itself is the cure for many ills:

Illness, you know, does not hinder me from walking; neither does anxiety. On the contrary, the more I walk, the better and stouter I become; and I believe if everybody were to regard the restlessness which anxiety creates, as a signal from nature to get up and contend with it in that manner, people would find the benefit of it. This is more particularly the case if they are lovers of Nature, as well as pupils of her, and have an eye for the beauties in which her visible world abounds.

He knows the history of the region, and there are plenty of references to Elizabeth and Charles II, as well as to local grandees that few modern readers will have heard of, but Hunt has a knack for shaping an anecdote to give it meaning regardless of the specifics of the historical background. He also chats with the coachmen and innkeepers, and gives them credit for being as sensitive and eager for "the good life" as any blueblood.

In one village he tours a church with an organ, and learns that the organist is the son of the parish clerk.

> When I asked his sister, a modest, agreeable-looking girl,
> who showed us the church, whether he could not favor us
> with a voluntary, she told me he was making hay ! What do
> you say to that?

Hunt presumes that the father too, was a day-laborer, and
had been organist before his son took over the job, "out of a
natural love of music." He then paints the following scene:

> I had fetched the girl from her tea. A decent-looking young
> man was in the room with her ; the door was open, exhibit-
> ing the homely comforts inside; a cat slept before it, on the
> cover of the garden well, and there was plenty of herbs and
> flowers, presenting altogether the appearance of a cottage
> nest.

At this point Hunt reflects on the role played by music in the
lives of these village people:

> I will be bound that their musical refinements are a great
> help to the enjoyment of all this; and that a general lift in
> their tastes, instead of serving to dissatisfy the poor, would
> have a reverse effect, by increasing the sum of their resources.

Arriving in the village of Streatham, where Samuel Johnson spent a great deal of time with his friends, the Thrales,
Hunt makes an effort to find someone with personal impressions of the great man. After a few misfires, he meets up
with "a decent-looking old man, with a sharp eye and a hale
countenance, who, with an easy, self-satisfied air, as if he
had worked enough in his time and was no longer under the
necessity of over-troubling himself, sat indolently cracking
stones in the road."

Among other bits of minutia, Hunt learns that Johnson
would sometimes "have his dinner brought out to him in the

park, and set on the ground; and while he was waiting for it, would lie idly, and cut the grass with a knife." According to Hunt's elderly informant, Dr. Johnson's manners were "very good-natured, and sometimes so childish, that people would have taken him for 'an idiot, like.'"

At another point in his ramble Hunt ponders the case of a local grandee, considered to be generous and kind by the villagers, who nevertheless prohibits access to the local churchyard (except on Sundays) because the path passs in front of his house. "How his act of power squares with his kindness, I do not know," Hunt remarks. "Very good-natured people are sometimes very fond of having their own way."

Hunt's curiosity seems boundless. He even goes so far as to read, and reflect on, the sentiments expressed on the gravestones he passes in the churchyards. Though the story is too complicated to describe in detail, after reviewing the facts related on one such headstone—a story that Hunt suspects his contemporaries would consider unduly sentimental—he delivers the following aside:

> *There is more friendship and virtue in the world than the world has yet got wisdom enough to know and be proud of; and few things would please me better than to travel all over England, and fetch out the records of it.*

In short, I like this guy: his temperament, his powers of observation, his easy-going style.

But I was disconcerted to discover that Hunt has developed a reputation as an irresponsible scoundrel. He is described by the discerning critic John Bayley as "a careless butterfly sort of man, abounding in fine feelings, who loved his fellow men and let them pick up the pieces."

But wait! Bayley isn't describing Leigh Hunt in this passage. He's describing Harold Skimpole, a character in the novel *Bleak House*. Dickens claimed he had drawn Skimpole as an exact likeness of his friend Hunt. I rather doubt it. The bio posted by the Poetry Foundation observes that Hunt produced, during the first sixty years of the nineteenth century, "a large body of poetry in a variety of forms: narrative poems, satires, poetic dramas, odes, epistles, sonnets, short lyrics, and translations from Greek, Roman, Italian, and French poems." He was the indefatigable publisher and editor of several liberal magazines, including the influential *Examiner*, in which he published early works of both Keats and Shelley. He also spent two years in prison as a result of one of his inflammatory political editorials.

The bio goes on to state that Hunt "has probably had more influence on the development of the personal essay than any other writer," and describes his *Autobiography* (1850) as "perhaps his best work and arguably the best autobiography of the century." In another on-line source we read that "his death was simply exhaustion."

He hardly sounds like a frivolous and conniving wastrel to me.

A Gorgeous Thaw

The sun came out after a blustery, rainy morning, and suddenly everyone was out on the street. I went out too, but only to hack down a few of the bushes under the windows outside the den.

"Hack down" might not be the proper phrase to describe this delicate and artful process, by which I succeed in taming the twelve-foot shrubs—forsythia, yellow-twig dogwood, and highbush cranberry—that have thrived in the six-foot space under those windows for thirty-odd years.

The theory is that if you cut back a shrub before the sap starts to run, adventitious buds will develop further down on the branches, and as it leafs out, the plant in question will become fuller and more shapely while also remaining shorter.

Most years I forget to do this. It takes a sunny Friday afternoon in mid-February when the temperature reaches 45 degrees to alert me to the task.

Meanwhile, Hilary went out to the street to chat with the neighbors. Stephan was walking his son Logan home from school, Brendan appeared from his garage to return a vase we'd given his wife, Sarah, along with some flowers, to cheer her up while she was convalescing from an operation. And Alice, who moved into the house next door only last October, joined the party because—why not?

Hilary and I then set out for a brief stroll through the neighborhood. A pale moon was visible, but we saw no turkeys in the trees, no deer tracks in the vanishing snow. We were both reminded of the joy felt by children listening to the sound of water running down the street and into the storm sewer grates. It excites the deepest recesses of one's being. We felt it ourselves. I found a twig and tossed it into the flow of melt-water, but it was too heavy—or the stream was too shallow, the current too slow.

A week ago the temperature was -24°. At that time we were two hundred miles north of here, but still. Yet I have little doubt that it will snow again more than once before we emerge into summer's garden.

But right now the sunlight hits the trees in a celebratory way, and it almost seems that the earth is starting to breathe again.

Snowy Owls

It's the time of year when we get excited about the return of the robins. I saw one the other day down by the railroad tracks that cross through Theodore Wirth Golf Course. Robins tend to hang out there all winter, but I hadn't seen one for months, and hearing that cheerful cluck as he flew overhead was a treat.

Winter birding is mostly occupied with a few species— woodpeckers, goldfinches, cardinals, chickadees, juncos, blue jays. There is usually one time during the winter, after or during a heavy snowfall, when the cardinals appear at the feeder *en masse*. During one such mid-afternoon storm in mid-January, I counted nine of them in the tree just beyond the deck. A pileated woodpecker pays our feeder a visit at least once every winter. Sometimes once a week.

The winter season is made more interesting by the arrival in northern Minnesota of arctic species, and this year some of them made their way farther south than usual. I saw my first-ever Bohemian waxwing on Park Point in Duluth in January, and during a visit with friends a few weeks ago to Itasca State Park, we walked right past a black-backed woodpecker who, heedless of the intrusion, continued to pound away at the bark of a sturdy red pine. I was hardly less smitten by an abandoned nest we passed hanging from a fork in a branch only a few feet off the ground. Maybe a red-eyed vireo?

Ducks are now passing through town, looking for open water. Hilary and I went down to the Bass Ponds a few days ago to find large numbers of common mergansers—one of our most majestic birds—and also quite a few hooded mergansers, which are among the most beautiful, along with five or six scaup. We spotted a kingfisher buzzing from one pond to the next—a true spring sighting. And several robins were clucking around, too.

We talked to the only other birder down there, and he asked us if we'd been to the airport to see the snowy owls.

"We went there yesterday," I replied, "but saw nothing except airplanes."

"Well, there were three of them there again this morning."

"Maybe we arrived too late," I said. *Maybe we just weren't trying hard enough*, I thought.

This morning, as I stepped out to get the newspaper, the air was calm and the sunrise was stunning. Hey! It was still early. And Sunday morning might be the best time of the week to visit the airport without worrying about the traffic.

So we got in the car and headed for the viewing lot on Cargo Road. Twenty minutes later we were standing on a picnic table, looking across a few runways at a snowy owl that was sitting on top of a flat-roofed building. Wow.

A man at the far end of the lot had pointed out the bird to us, though we would have spotted it before long. "I've seen three of them this morning. There's one over by Gate 5, and another by that yellow pole—see it, in front of that red truck?" (It was the same man we'd seen at the Bass Ponds the previous day.)

We watched the owls preen themselves and swivel their heads from side to side. One of them eventually took to the air and flew right past us like a fuzzy white barrel with wings, on his way to a nearby rooftop, where he landed on a railing but soon disappeared beyond the lip of the roof.

Astounding birds. Huge. Inscrutable. Nomadic. And their view of the airport runways is unique. They spent much of their lives in the treeless tundra; I think the airport reminds them of home.

On our way back into town, we exited the freeway at Diamond Lake Road, looking for a bakery. We were headed for Patisserie 46 but pulled in at Sun Street Breads at 48th and Nicollet. It smelled like Paris inside, and it's always a delight to see people out and about on a Sunday morning—savvy South Minneapolis people, who perhaps meet their friends here every week.

Spring

Easter and the Pelicans

My dad never joined in family conversations much, preferring to listen stolidly from the sidelines in the time-honored Swedish tradition, but when he did say something, it was invariably brief and to the point. I recall a family discussion about religion around the dining-room table one evening back in my high school days. I was saying, "Religion is sort of repetitive," to which he replied, "Well, nature is also repetitive."

On the face of things, that's true. We see the same succession of the same things, year in and year out: the buds on the maple tree swell, the red-winged blackbirds return. But the interval between such events—an entire year—gives us a long time to forget. Meanwhile, the progress of the seasons is so complex and the range of variations so diverse that it's far from predictable.

That explains, I guess, why I still find it worthwhile to head down river, year after year, to see which birds are coming toward us in the opposite direction on their way to breeding grounds up north. We never know quite what we're going to meet up with.

We spotted fifty-odd species during our two-day Easter trip. Some were residents that we'd been seeing all winter— downies, hairies, chickadees, mallards, cardinals, crows. Some were déclassé specimens that few observers are going to get excited about, beyond the simple fact that they've returned: grackles, starlings, turkey vultures, red-winged blackbirds. (Others may disagree, but I would rather see a blue jay than a crow.) And we did see a single bluebird on our trip—the spring avant garde, as it were.

The more thrilling species that pass through at this time of year—and I mean thrilling—are the waterfowl. They tend to be beautiful and they tend to travel in mixed groups, which creates the impression, probably illusory, that they've formed communities sharing an arctic destination, thus giving us a sense of a complex, geographically vast, and mysterious life about which we know very little. Day by day, we never know precisely which ducks we're going to see.

On our road trip down the Mississippi, Hilary and I saw plenty of common mergansers, though the word "common" does little to evoke those immaculate and handsome white bodies. We also saw some goldeneyes, alert and compact, and seven or eight shovelers, whose oversized bills hardly detract from their lovely green and rufus flanks. The ring-necked ducks, with their proudly-stiff heads, look like aristocratic cousins of the scaup.

I have a fondness for gadwalls, large and subtle to the point of being nondescript. We saw exactly one. We also saw one green-winged teal, too far away to appreciate fully even with the scope. Canvasbacks, ruddy ducks, redheads, pintails? No such luck.

For non-birders, the star of any trip down the Mississippi will likely be the bald eagle. We saw close to sixty such birds, either soaring or resting in the trees. Swans are also present in numbers, though they look less impressive sitting on a big slab of ice than when they're floating dreamily in a narrow river lined with willows two hundred miles to the north.

More impressive than either of these birds, to my mind, is the pelican. These birds are often overlooked because they migrate in large, concentrated flocks, often far above the ground. Our most thrilling sighting of the trip was of a large flock of pelicans moving toward us in a long undulating line.

We were on foot, well out on Kiep's Island Dike Road in Trempealeau National Wildlife Refuge, a few miles north of La Crosse, Wisconsin. We watched them approach against the distant, dark gray bluff-side, wings beating in rhythm. It looked like a military display, or better yet, a Chinese ink scroll painting. At one point their formation seemed to break apart in confusion; I think they were examining the fifteen swans resting out on the ice a few hundred yards beneath them. They soon regrouped, and as the string of mostly white creatures passed overhead I counted seventy birds.

This trip was a birthday present of sorts for Hilary, and I had scoped out all the best restaurants in La Crosse, prepared for any celebratory taste or whim. But we had made the mistake of stopping at JJ's Barbeque in Nelson for lunch.

"Are you here for the brunch?" the woman behind the counter asked. "It's $11.95, all you can eat, and it includes coffee and juice."

The food was pretty good. They smoke the meat out back. But of course, there was too much of it. So once we'd checked into our hotel in La Crosse, and driven up to Grandma's Bluff to watch the sun go down, and spotted our first red-winged blackbird in the park near the university campus, we were happy to crash back in our hotel room with some cheese and crackers and a bottle of wine.

Plenty of old buildings remain standing in downtown La Crosse, which is a mixed blessing. Most of them are occupied and open for business, but the wide range of signs and colors painted on the bricks gives the neighborhood a rundown look. Perhaps the major eyesore is the Bodega Brew Pub, situated at a prime location where the street makes a slight bend. It advertises the availability of 420 beers, and thirty or forty empty bottles are gathering dust in the window display. On a gray Monday morning in March, the place doesn't look inviting.

The coffee-shop next door was open but dark and almost empty when we walked by. A passage connects it to the Pearl Street used book store—an asset to any urban scene—and the shop across the street might contain the largest collection of rubber stamps in the world.

Other nearby shops include Kate's Pizza Amorè, Fayze's pine-paneled café and bakery, and a branch of the Duluth Trading Company.

Down at the riverfront things are different: everything has been spiffed up or torn down. An upscale wine shop and Piggy's smoked meats restaurant occupies a handsomely retro-fitted nineteenth-century warehouse. The Radisson Hotel and convention center, along with its huge parking lot, dominates a block or two, and Viterbo University seems to have invested heavily in trim new brick buildings. A robust fine arts center stands on one corner, and though the trees are bare and the grass is still brown or gray, the string of riverside parks looked very nice from our seventh-story eyrie at the hotel.

The next morning, on a whim, we drove out to the Shrine of Our Lady of Guadalupe, which is tucked into the hills a few miles southeast of town. It turned out to be a big complex, complete with a restaurant, bakery, and gift shop adjacent to the parking lot.

Following a path that wound up the hill into the trees, we came upon a stone building housing an enormous pyramid of blue glasses, each of which contained a votive-candle. A hundred yards further on, a large brick church, classically simple in design, stood in a clearing. From the plaza the path returned to the woods, continuing upward past the stations of the cross and then a rosary walk.

We were the only people there except for a grounds keeper on a golf cart who opened the chapel for us and a tall young man named Brother Joe, whom we saw in his coarse gray hooded habit, scurrying around the church with a vacuum cleaner.

We had plenty of time to soak up the spirit of sanctity that pervaded the place. The paintings, the sculpture, the ceramic tiles—they were all far better and less kitschy than I'd imagined they would be. In fact, the setting reminded me of monasteries Hilary and I visited years ago in Tuscany and Umbria, also during the frigid days of early spring. How much of the mood was due to the art, and how much to the solitude, the silence, the hills, the woods, the company? Who can say?

And to top it all off, a tufted titmouse—a bird we never see as far north as Minneapolis—started singing away in the woods nearby. Less a song than a rich but piercing and insistent two-note call, repeated again and again, it seemed like a sonic crystallization of the deep, chilly morning.

The Art of the
Wasted Weekend

These last few days have put my wasted-day artistry to the test. Hilary is out of town, and I have quite a bit of time on my hands. Sure, I have books to edit and a website to update. I also came up with a List of Things I Might Do while Hilary is Out of Town, to wit:

- Reseed the front yard
- build a new planter for the deck
- transplant some hostas and violets out into the fringe of the back yard where nothing seems to grow except moss
- re-attach the spice rack to the kitchen wall
- organize the CDs (an all-day job)

But I can't help feeling that I'm spinning my wheels. These expanses of solitude are a rare gift, and they ought to build like afternoon thunderheads, moving through spells of abject torment to sudden flashes of insight.

It doesn't seem to be happening. Here are a few of my recent "reflections." You be the judge:

– A pleasant morning picking up some groceries at Cub for a quinoa/black bean salad, some manure and top-soil at Ace hardware.

– I just got done transplanting some hosta and periwinkle. Nothing is more fun than that. Then I fetched an old copy of *Making Things Grow Outdoors* by Thalassa Cruso from the basement. Now largely forgotten, Cruso was once considered the Julia Child of the gardening world, perhaps because she had a TV show. When I first read her I admired her style, conversational yet slightly elevated.

– It's a hot afternoon. I'm on the deck with a glass of fizzy water enlivened by a splash of Campari. I played tennis briefly with a friend at noon—horrible courts in Bryn Mawr. Still, it was good to get out into the day.

– A quiet evening. Dipping into the musty copy of Gabriel Marcel's *Creative Fidelity* that I got in the mail the other day, I come upon this remark:

> *I think I may say without exaggeration that my whole philosophical career has been devoted to the production—I dislike using that physical term—of currents whereby life can be reborn in regions of the mind which have yielded to apathy and are exposed to decomposition.*

And a few pages later:

> *Philosophy provides the means for experience to become aware of itself, to apprehend itself—but at what level of experience? And how can such a hierarchy be established or defined?...We must distinguish not only degrees of clarification but degrees of intimacy with oneself and with one's surroundings—with the universe itself.*

– It's time to quit being disappointed by the fact that you're not doing anything interesting with your free time. You can no longer claim it's because you have too many commitments. It must be because your mind is a BLANK!

It's getting dark, a little windy, as if a storm were approaching, maybe a tornado on a hot evening like this. The branches are going a little wild.

– We must not forget how beautiful the trees were up north, pale yellow, just leafing out. The winding road on the way up to the top of Giant's Ridge. Deep pines, pale aspens. Hints of Colorado.

– Now I hear thunder. Time to shut down and unplug the computer.

– It's raining harder now. Moderately. I've got the door cracked open a few inches. It's cooled off quite a bit out there. Gentle thunder. Deep thunder. But the sky looks lighter in the west. A good rain.

– When I dip into Marcel, I feel that his methods are sound and his conclusions are subtle and valid. When I dip into Kierkegaard, I feel that he's just talking to hear himself talk. He relishes the feverish cleverness, the irony, but isn't taking the issues at hand seriously.

Am I taking the issues seriously? Not really.

What *are* the issues at hand?

* * *

Up at 5:15. Well, I went to bed at 9. Books at my bedside: *Concluding Unscientific Post-Script*, William Gass's *Tests of Time*, Marcel's *Creative Fidelity*, *Everybody's Pepys*. But nothing held my interest except the yellowing bookmark I found in the Kierkegaard. "Discount Records $12.99, at 10:41 a.m. on March 16, 1985."

CDs weren't widely available then. Someone bought an LP. Was it me?

Max Frisch might have spun an entire novel out of that receipt. Which reminds me that I have never read *Wilderness of Mirrors* or *I'm Not Stiller*, though both books are sitting right here on the shelf.

It rained all night, as far as I can tell. I ought to get out and spread some grass seed on those bare spots. No task seems more futile to me than over-seeding a wretched lawn, but it might be more pleasant to do it barefoot, before the sun comes up. (I have heard that grass seed germinates better under those conditions.)

* * *

Marcel: "The mystery [of the life to come] is of such a nature that its rejection deprives human life not only of its principal dimension but also, little by little, of its entire significance and depth."

* * *

A beautiful male cardinal has been jumping around the lip of the bird bath for the last five minutes, warily turning his head in every direction. Just now he took the plunge, splashed around in the pool for about twenty seconds, and then flew off. For myself, I'm warily circling around any number of projects but remain unengaged, unwilling to take the plunge into one thing and give up the likelihood of pursuing something else.

No sooner do I write these words than I leap up with determination to continue work on the wooden planter I'm making to replace the one that rotted out here on the deck. The minute I head into the garage to get the lumber the miasma lifts and my life once again has purpose. After sawing through two 1 x 12s, I'm reminded that the last time I did this I threw my back out. Well, that's enough for today.

* * *

Right around 4 o'clock the mood changes. Whatever you have or haven't done, you're entering a freer zone, beyond tasks or apologies. It's like getting home from work.

* * *

Marcel again, in delicately humorous mode: "Just when we want an exact statement as to what 'spirit' really is, people generally remain vague to the point of impoliteness."

Marcel's meditations on death are subtle, but I don't think they would mean much to someone who's actually dying. I'm thinking of my dad, who lost his capacity for speech in his final months. In the end he was reduced to being wheeled around in a wheel chair with a bewildered look on his face, and our job was to do our best to preserve his dignity, to remind him who he had been, and perhaps still was.

Marcel rejects Heidegger's famous theory of "being toward death," arguing that it's based on a primitive and false notion of the relationship between "my body" and "my self." At a later point he observes that "the man of authentic existence in Heidegger's mind is not the man who truly lives with other people, but rather a man 'who knows true life only in dealing with himself."

Marcel's own views can be reduced to four concepts—attentiveness, availability, participation, and hope—all of which flourish in human company. I was going to say "in society" but society is an abstraction that tends to depersonalize things. Marcel elevates hope to the level of a theological virtue. I suspect he sees it as an attitude or orientation or personality rather than a theory about living to be either confirmed or invalidated.

Many years ago a friend of mine told me: Old age begins at 80. At the time I had no idea what he meant—I would have proposed 65 as a good threshold—but he was a cardiologist and had seen lots of very old people. He merely meant that at that age everything begins to fall apart. It's a matter of physiology.

The essayist Patricia Hampl enjoys telling about her dad, who divided life into three phases: youth, middle age, and "You look good!" But "You look good!" is often more than mere flattery or dissimulation. When we meet up with someone we've known and loved for decades, our vision extends beyond physiology to encompass a rich history and a glow of enduring affection. It's true. You *do* look good.

* * *

I seem to be settling in, in so far as I'm still awake at 9:30. Hoping to keep the "spirit" alive, this afternoon I declined a friend's invitation to sample a few rare wines from Columbia and also deferred a proposal for a round of golf to next week.

* * *

But now the sun has come out and the day's heating up. Sitting on the deck in mid-morning (a cooper's hawk just flew by fifty feet overhead), drinking coffee, listening to the goldfinches chatter, and watching a bee hunt in vain for the last remaining flower on the dogwood bushes a few feet away. The line of emerging sunlight creeps across the deck toward my shady spot here against the dining room wall. The sky is a pale blue, the wind is rustling in the trees, the coffee has grown cold, and I'm reading Novalis, *The Novices of Sais*, where he writes:

> *The capriciousness of nature seems of itself to fall within the idea of human personality, which is apparently best grasped in the form of a human creature. That is why poetry has been the favorite instrument of true friends of nature, and the spirit of nature has shown most radiantly in poems. When we read and hear true poems, we feel the*

movement of nature's inner reason and, like its celestial embodiment, we dwell in it and hover over it at once.

A few pages on, Novalis puts this speech into the mouth of one of his characters:

To everything that man undertakes he must give his undivided attention, his self; once he has done this, miraculously thoughts arise, or new kinds of perceptions, which appear to be nothing more than delicate, abrupt movements of a colored pencil, or strange contractions and figurations of an elastic liquid. From the point where he has transfixed the impression, they spread in all directions with a living mobility and carry his self with them.

At this point Novalis heads off down a path that scholars might consider an elaboration (or criticism) of Fichte's thought, but I have neither the background nor an interest in such things.

Often he can stop this movement at the onset by dividing his attention or letting it wander at random, for thoughts seem to be nothing other than emanations and effects which the self induces all around it in that elastic medium, or the refractions of the self in that medium, or in general a strange game that the waves of this ocean play with the rigidity of concentration. Strange to say, it is only through this play that man becomes aware of his uniqueness, his specific freedom; it seems to him then as though he were waking from a deep sleep, as though he had just begun to be at home in the universe, as though the light of day had just broken in upon his inner world.

Now a small white butterfly flutters by, the size of a quarter. I've gone inside to get a hat—the sunlight will soon be upon me. The goldfinches have vanished, the chickadees have arrived. A red-bellied woodpecker shrieks from nearby. Always cardinals. Now a house finch!

And now a train whistle, of all things.

I'll be heading out soon to a meeting. But now I see a tiny fly, the size of a piece of rice, on the back of the chair here beside the one I'm sitting on. Its abdomen glistens a deep turquoise, inlaid with rings of gold.

* * *

Saturday. An early morning bike ride around the sixteen-mile loop at Elm Creek, before the day gets hot. It was almost chilly in the shadowy stretches. The chokecherries are in bloom. Lots of birds singing: yellow-throats, red-eyed vireos, five or six veerys, an oriole or two, and at least twenty clay-colored sparrows. I brought my binoculars and stopped once or twice to ferret one out—they sit on bushes out in the fields, usually at eye level—but I never saw one.

The next stop on my morning outing was the bridge over Bassett Creek a few blocks from our house. That's where I sample water clarity as a "citizen scientist" for the DNR. I checked the creek yesterday because of the rain, which tends to stir things up, and the reading was 22 cm, one of the worst ever. This morning, on the other hand, it had already risen to the best reading, +100 cm. That surprised me.

It has also surprised me again and again, over the years, that as people pass by me on the bridge, they don't seem the least bit curious about what I'm doing. Of course, they're often engaged in their own conversations. But if I were to spot someone standing on a bridge with a long plastic tube and a yellow bucket on a rope, I'd be likely to stop and ask them what was going on.

This morning, things were different. While I was lowering the bucket into the creek, a young man rode up on his bike and stopped. Maybe that's because (as I soon learned) he works as a geologist for the DNR. His name was Ron. He had a long last name that I didn't quite catch.

"Is that Romanian?" I asked.

"Close. Guess again."

"Polish?"

"You're almost there ... Lithuanian."

A minute later his wife arrived pushing a baby in a stroller equipped with an umbrella, from which I deduced that they had not come far. That also explained why he'd stopped on the bridge.

"Do you live nearby?" I asked.

"We live in Robbinsdale, just north of here on Wirth Parkway."

"I live up that way, too, by St. Margaret Mary Church. Right at the top of the hill."

Then I said, "Is Robbinsdale getting cool, or what?"

He smiled. "We like to think there are some businesses going in that care about quality."

"Well, you've got that brewery, Wicked—" I couldn't think of the name.

"The Wicked Wort."

"Yeah, and then Travail, of course." I thought I'd pronounced the name properly, in the French manner, but evidently that's not how you're supposed to say it; he corrected me.

"I haven't eaten there since they started issuing tickets," I said. "The food was good, but the music was too LOUD."

Ron just smiled.

Just then his wife chimed in: "There's a new place downtown called Marta's. They have a breakfast bowl that's to die for."

Another couple had come up beside me, and as Ron and his wife headed off and I began pouring the bucket of water into the tube, the man said, "Turbidity."

For a split-second I wasn't sure what "turbidity" meant. I like to think I'm measuring how *clear* the water is, rather than how dirty, but I suppose you could just as well put it the other way around.

"This creek has really gotten cleaned up," the man said. "You never used to see fish in here."

"Mostly what you see now are suckers," I said.

"But there's some shiners down there right now. Do you see those flashes of light near that log? They were never here before. They've cleaned up the creek all the way into Crystal. Do you know about that project?"

"Well, I've seen the big signs they put up. There was one right there in front of that willow last year." I pointed. "And I've seen the embankment rolls they put down and the rock walls they built just upstream from here. On the other hand, thirty years ago that lagoon was full of water most of the time. Now it's just a muddy island after during heavy rain."

"Maybe that's the idea," he said. "Water collects there during heavy rain rather than flooding over the parkway like it used to do." Good point.

Just then a spotted sandpiper flew past. He arched back and forth over the creek in front of us several times. A beautiful flier, always keeping his wings low and stiff.

"There's a spotted sandpiper," I said.

"A what?" the man's wife said.

"You won't believe what I've seen here, three times," I said. They both looked at me.

"A mink."

I don't think they believed me.

* * *

My next stop was Eat My Words Bookstore, just across the Mississippi in Northeast. I'd been carrying a box of books in the back seat for quite a while. "Scott will be in soon," his daughter said. "Just put the box on the table over there."

Before leaving I took a quick look around the shop. As usual, the titles that jumped out at me were the ones I sold to Scott months or years ago. Should I buy back that copy of *Jerusalem Delivered* that I bought in Santa Fe but never even glanced at before reselling? He wants $5.

* * *

My final mission took me to the opposite end of town, to North St. Paul, which might well be considered the Robbinsdale of the metro's East Side. Friends had been telling me for years about an eccentric wine merchant who dealt in "bin ends" that he bought wholesale and sold at a discount at a little shop called Bright Wines. But "shop" isn't the right word to describe his business. Wines sit in stacked cases or on home-made pine shelves. The space has no windows and it's dark inside, but that doesn't matter much because prices aren't marked.

It's a very "personal" operation. (Marcel would have approved.) Here's how it works. I step inside and a disembodied voice from the office says, "Hello." A tallish man appears with a friendly, squarish face and a thick head of hair lined with a few fine streaks of gray. A youthful fifty? I shake his hand.

"I'm on your email list but I've never been here before."

"Welcome," he replies. "I'm Dave."

"I was looking over your offerings, and I'm interest in the Phantom—"

"Oh, the reserve chardonnay from Bogle. It's right here."

"And what about that red from Languedoc you mentioned in the newsletter?"

"Oh, yes. Parker gave it 91 points. You'll love it."

Bottles begin to go into a box. By the time we're through I've assembled a case consisting of Mas Champart Saint-Chinian Causse de Bousquet 2012, Brunelli Poggio Apricale Toscane 2106, Mâcon-Chaintre Reserve des Rochers 2015, Bila-Haut Cote de Roussillon 2105, Clos de Fleur Sonoma County Chardonnay 2102, and the 2016 Bogle Clarksburg Phantom Chardonnay that I mentioned earlier.

If you've never heard of these wines, don't worry. I haven't either. The hope is that the Rosso de Montelcino will have a hint of the much more expensive Brunello from that region, and that the Mâcon-Chaintre will be a step above the more generic Mâcon-Village.

In any event, they sure *sound* pretty. And in case you're wondering, the prices are reasonable. I might have avoided the Clos de Fleur if I'd known it was six years old. Then again, it was the cheapest of the lot. Take a chance!

Driving through North St. Paul brought back memories from my youth. The village I grew up in, Mahtomedi, is nearby. My mother used to drive me to North St. Paul to get my jeans and shoes at Miller's. When Shopper's City appeared a few miles down the road, it was a big deal.

Both of those stores are long gone, but the town's main street now has more trees and perhaps more bars, though it's hard for me to tell—at age thirteen, I wasn't paying much attention. As I crossed Highway 36 I went past the high school, where I once played a doubles tennis match on hardwood gym floors in front of the entire team. The ball skids a lot more on that surface, and the North St. Paul team had been practicing on it for weeks.

Ah, the humiliations of youth.

Walks in (Drizzle) Beauty

Walk in beauty: so the Navajo advise us, though it's not that easy to do. Yet sometimes it seems that beauty walks in us. Or all around us. We try to worm our way in.

Hilary had six or seven friends over for book club Friday night. That's a good time for me to get out of the house for a while. I hauled my bike down to Lake of the Isles and did a few circuits. Everyone was out in shorts and T-shirts, on paddleboards, traversing the lake in colorful kayaks and canoes, walking dogs, pushing strollers, or sprawled on the grass reading books.

Then on to Calhoun, where I parked on the west side of the lake, just across from the volleyball courts, and pulled out a copy of Roberto Calasso's *Ardor*.

The Vedic world [he writes] *involved a cult, closely bound up with texts of extreme complexity and an intoxicating plant. A state of awareness became the pivot around which turned thousands and thousands of meticulously codified ritual acts. A mythology, as well as the boldest speculation, arose out of the fateful and dramatic encounter between a liturgy and rapture.*

I was having a hard time concentrating (maybe you were, too) when suddenly it occurred to me that I was only a few blocks from a shop I'd read about in the paper that sold Minnesota-grown plants such as turtlehead and cup plant. Thus I abandoned the mysterious life of northern India circa 2000 B.C. and penetrated ever deeper into the hardly less mysterious life of the Linden Hills neighborhood.

The shop was nowhere to be found, but a few blocks down the way I passed 44 France Wines & Spirits, which I hadn't visited for at least fifteen years. I parked and went inside. I was looking over the bargain bins when, out of the corner of my eye, I noticed that my old friend Fran was standing right next to me. I play tennis with her husband from time to time, and I happened to know he was in Norway visiting his brother. She told me a little about how his trip was going, and about how much she was enjoying her week of solitude, though she wasn't relishing it as much as she'd hoped. That horrible thing called work kept getting in the way.

When I asked her about the plant shop I was looking for, she said: "I don't think there's a business like that near here. But there is a woman who sets out some things on planks along the sidewalk on weekends."

THE NEXT MORNING Hilary and I headed back down to the lakes. We circled Isles and Calhoun by bike and wandered the rock garden north of Harriet, but turned back to the car when it began to drizzle.

Back on 44th Street, we found the woman with her small selection of plants out on the sidewalk and bought a few. She only sells plants native to Minnesota, so she had the white turtleheads, but not the purple.

The morning was gray but the drizzle was a mere tickle, so light as to be refreshing. A perfect day to plant. And not only that. After a good deal of debate, we decided the time had come to repair the crumbling border to the garden. It's been deteriorating for years, but I was holding fast to the idea that the best solution might be to allow it to disappear entirely, thus naturalizing the space. Once the logs had rotted we could create a far less boxy look simply by shifting a few plants around. One benefit to this plan was that it required almost no work. The drawback was that it might take a decade or more for Mother Nature to complete her part of the operation, during which time the garden would continue to look a little shabby.

Hilary pulled a log out from under the deck that had been there since we moved in. It was a little bent, but it fit the space nicely. My job would be to drive some spikes through the log to hold it in place. And that, I knew, would be much easier if I pre-drilled the holes. And that would be much easier, I was sure, if my drill actually worked.

Ninety minutes later I was holding a brand-new bright green Ryobi drill in my hand with which I cheerily ground a few holes through the replacement log. (I found that the drill worked even better, and stopped emitting an unpleasant burning smell, when it was set on forward rather than reverse.) The salesman at Home Depot had done an exemplary job of explaining what was likely to be wrong with my old drill, and why it might make sense simply to get it fixed—they don't make them like they used to. Then, with nary a hint of condescension, he patiently reviewed the relative merits of the corded and battery-powered models currently available. In fact, he was so personable and articulate that I left the store absolutely convinced I'd made a brilliant choice.

The spikes I bought had looked a little big in the store, but they also proved to be perfectly suited to the task at hand.

The gray weather lingered throughout the weekend, and so did the unhurried pace, which added to the pleasure of planting things. You look over the garden spaces in a kind of mental fog as your mind reviews all the plants that have died or disappeared in previous years. You envision sure-fire winners such as zinnia and cleome for the sunnier patches out front. You ponder bee-, butterfly-, and bird-friendly native choices and wonder where you might find them for sale. You wonder what you might divide, and what you might remove entirely. And there are the ever-present violets and ferns to manage.

The weekend was pleasantly punctuated by a birthday party, dinner guests, and even a film—an appropriately rural remake of *Far from the Madding Crowd*. By Monday morning the sun had returned. During a trip to the farmer's market, our second of the weekend, I picked up some pre-started morning glories, and on the way home I snagged a red-twigged dogwood at the supermarket to plant on the far side of the house, where two diseased elm trees are no longer with us.

Throughout the weekend we lived on tomatoes, fresh basil, garlic, and olive oil on toasted slices of French bread.

In Minnesota, spring lasts about three weeks. Summer is almost here.

Prom Night

W hat brings you to this neck of the woods?" said the woman behind the desk at the Country Inn in Two Harbors.

"Birding," I replied.

That wasn't exactly true. Hilary and I have gotten into the habit of taking a week off at about this time of year—mid-May—and my birthday also happens to fall conveniently within the range. We roam the countryside exploring new sights, revisiting old favorites, eating a lot of cheese and crackers, and camping or sleeping in motels depending on weather, availability, and whim.

But the fact that many unusual birds are passing through the state on their way to nesting grounds farther north—birds that we haven't seen in their prime, if at all, since last year's spring migration—makes the trip that much more interesting.

We usually head south down the Mississippi Valley, but this year the forecast in Preston (south) was 46 degrees and rain, while in Duluth (north) it was 65 degrees and sun. The question was, had the warblers gotten that far north yet?

"Birding," I said to the woman behind the desk, then added, "But there aren't any birds!" That wasn't precisely true, either. We'd seen some very fine little creatures, including one spectacular close-up of a magnolia warbler during a hike through Banning State Park, where we'd stopped on the drive up.

After getting settled in our room we went down to the harbor and were surprised to find that the parking lot was full of cars. It looked like a wedding event, but the gowns were so diverse and the vehicles so many that we soon rejected that idea. A woman sitting on a bench told us: "It's prom night. Everyone comes down here to take pictures."

Indeed, there were lots of teenage girls in fancy dresses, lots of shoulders exposed and midriffs covered by sheer garments. The poor girls were probably freezing. The boys, as usual, wore a less imaginative (but warmer) array of suits and ties. Parents, friends, and siblings were also present with cameras. I even took a picture myself.

Then I saw a yellow bird fly into the single leafless bush between the mass of teens and the breakwater. A Nashville warbler! Beautiful white eye-ring.

While I was looking at it, Hilary said, "Look. There's a horned grebe." It had just popped up from the depths of the harbor.

Just then I noticed a Lincoln sparrow sharing the bush with the Nashville warbler: beautiful breast, a band of pale gold under the sharp dark streaks.

We headed off across the slabs of rock and I soon spotted a sparrow hopping around in a clump of last year's tall grasses. He had a yellowish wash in the streaks above his eye: a Savannah sparrow. That's a common bird, but I rarely see one.

We made our way along the shore keeping to the shelter of wooded fringe above the shelves of rock. It was cold, and there wasn't much activity, but as we rounded the bend we noticed a group of twenty-odd ducks pretty far out to sea. Long-tailed ducks?

Yes. And one of them, off by himself, had drifted fairly close to shore, from which point we could see his exotic plumage clearly.

By the time we got back to the parking lot the prom-goers had dispersed, leaving behind a few young boys and old men trying to make the most of the fishing opener by casting from shore.

Weddings are joyous events. Prom night? Perhaps slightly less so. How many couples will last the weekend? The next two years? Right now it doesn't matter. Who will become mayor, who will move to the Cities, who will find herself folding clothes at the local laundromat to make ends meet? It doesn't matter. It's the excitement of the moment, the sense of participation, the drama of the social group and the expectation of a long, wild, and perhaps romantic evening ahead.

Maybe the long-tailed ducks have an easier time: find a mate within the floating mass of chattering kindred spirits, raise a brood in the Arctic, spend the winter vacationing together—a package tour—on the open ocean. Repeat.

I ought to say something more about the beautiful hike we took along the Quarry Trail at Banning State Park. There were few leaves on the trees, and that made it easier to see the warblers, which included not only the magnolia warbler but also several black-and-whites, palms, and myrtles. The trail follows a ridge above the Kettle River past an abandoned sandstone quarry. We took a spur farther downstream to the top of the whitewater at Hell's Gate.

Buddy Snow, a member of my Boy Scout troop, lost his life there when I was in junior high school. He was canoeing with his dad, it was early spring, the water was frigid. Buddy was older than me, I didn't know him at all, though I knew his sister well.

As a teen I felt there was something awful and mysterious and yet sacred about the event—the evident finality of it all. That might seem too obvious to mention, but when you're a kid such feelings are rare. And that lingering feeling lent a somber, almost metaphysical quality to the dark and fast-moving yet strangely beautiful and unruffled water we were looking at now, half a century later.

Locust Petals

White petals of the black locust tree litter the garden and the deck, like confetti from a grand celebration we weren't invited to. It's impossible to see the blossoms themselves on the branch without binoculars, the tree is so tall. For twenty years I thought it was the neighbor's tree, deep in the woods, obscure and last to leaf out. Well, who really owns a tree?

As I sit here on the deck, soaking up the bright sun and exquisitely cool air, I'm thinking I might start up a pagoda dogwood farm.

We got our volunteer dogwood by chance (I guess that's what a "volunteer" is) from one-time neighbors Chris and Julie, with the help of the local chipmunks, no doubt. Chris had a thick head of hair and a maniacal grin. He liked The Who and wished he could party more. Julie, shy and near anorexic, spent a lot of time with her mother. Eventually they had a child and moved to Edina.

I spotted the sprout under the bedroom window one spring day. Now it's thirty feet tall, and three of its youngins are developing here and there out in the yard. We've given a few away.

Every spring I catch sight of the chipmunks venturing out on the delicate branches to harvest the berries with feverish daring and precision.

Janio, our neighbor to the other side, is a bachelor. He teaches at the local high school. One day recently, in a fit of good humor, I agreed to help him remove the buckthorn from the woods that separates our yards. I suppose it was the right thing to do, but it blew a few holes in the privacy screen.

"My sister's friend is a landscape designer," he told me. "She'll help me figure out what to plant there to create a new screen." But Janio doesn't seem too concerned about the plant life hereabouts. He's got other things on his mind.

A few days after we had this conversation, I noticed that the forsythia in our front yard had sent out a substantial sucker. I dug it up and replanted it in the disturbed soil where the buckthorn had been, along with a two-foot chunk of root. The plant is gangly, but three weeks later it's still green, and it looks to be doing fine.

As I tamped down the soil around the plant, I was reminded that we'd gotten that shrub from the woman who lived next door when we moved it, thirty-odd years ago. Cliff and Jan were among the neighborhood's original residents. A childless couple, they'd been living here for forty years by the time we arrived. Cliff worked for the phone company. Jan volunteered in the wildflower garden at the University Landscape Arboretum, where she was often given the opportunity to bring home cuttings from the experimental plant stock. She once told me she had twenty-nine varieties of hosta in her back yard. And I'm sure the redbud at the corner of their house, right next to our driveway, is one of the oldest in the state.

One day I ran into Jan out on the driveway and she offered me a clump of roots from the forsythia she was tidying up. At the time, I didn't know what a forsythia was.

"You know, the yellow flowers. First bloom of spring."

"Oh, yeah," I lied. "Sure. I'd be delighted. Thank you."

"Don't thank me for the plant," she replied. "Just thank me for the labor of digging it up."

Now there's a gnomic remark. I puzzled over it for years. I still do.

Half a life later, the forsythia is returning home to the other side of the lot line.

Cliff and Jan used to go bowling once a week. "I don't much like to bowl," she told me once with a chuckle, "but if I stopped going, we wouldn't have anything in common." She delivered the remark without rancor, out of a deep yet somehow chipper melancholy that she'd probably lived with throughout her life.

In any case, she was exaggerating. Cliff, too, liked to garden. He looked after the roses and the lawn, and managed their three-stage composting system, while she handled everything else. Not long after the two of them moved in, back in the Korean War era, Cliff planted five Colorado blue spruce—one-dollar seedlings—that served as a privacy fence between our two back yards for several decades. A few years after planting them he severed the roots with a shovel to encourage them to go deeper, thus stabilizing the trees, or so he thought.

I told that story to a master gardener at the farmers' market just last week and she said, "Well, all he did was bonsai the tree. Anyway, they don't recommend planting blue spruce in Minnesota any more. Too humid."

Those trees are now sixty feet tall. I wouldn't call them bonsai. It's true, one of them blew down in a storm a few years ago—so much for deep roots—and Janio had a second one removed this spring. It was dead. The other three are doing fine, though the branches are bare to a height of thirty feet.

One of our great gardening challenges is finding things that will grow underneath these towering spruce. Buckthorn, honeysuckle, and other invasives seem to do the best. Wild grapes. And best of all, Canadian elderberry. If it's green, we'll take it.

Jan was a wonderful neighbor, but in later years she had eye trouble and wore boxy wrap-around sunglasses when working out in the yard. The year Cliff died, I asked her (tactlessly, it seems to me now) where she was going to go for Christmas. "I suppose I'll be with Cliff's family," she said. "His brother lives right down the street." Then she gave a sweet little laugh and added: "I don't know if they like me, but I guess I'm part of the family by now."

Bicycles and Trout

We went to southeast Minnesota to catch the migrating warblers, and we met them head on at Hok-Si-La, Frontenac, and Forestville.

But we also met up with some interesting people pursuing entirely different objectives.

On Friday night we checked into a motel in Red Wing to escape the inclement weather, and the next morning we ran into two oddly-dressed gentlemen in the breakfast room. One of them was wearing tweed knickers and yellow-and-black argyle socks. Hilary told me later: "I had the passing thought that they might be going to a clown convention."

They were, in fact, from Winnipeg, and they were in town to participate in the Lake Pepin 3-Speed Tour. Here is a bit from the website I dug up just now:

> *To gain a better perspective, here is a list of things we leave behind: derailleurs, lycra, target heart rates, SPD, SIS, STI, HRM, XTR, etc. There will be no sprinting, spinning, drafting nor will there be any carbon fibre, drillium, eludium or unobtanium. Please note we are not advocating being a retro-grouch or ridicule those with alloy handlebars but instead we are asking you to strip away all you know modern cycling to be and hop aboard your £5 Thrift Store Raleigh and come with. Leave your lycra and Johnny-Rebel competitive spirit at home and instead, bring your sense of adventure.*

The elder of the two men had a warm, toothy smile and a silver-gray flattop. At one point he held up a medal that was hanging around his neck on a ribbon. "I still hold the seventy-and-over time trial record for Manitoba," he informed us proudly.

But speed is not the thing for this two-day, eighty-five-mile tour around Lake Pepin. You need to have a vintage bike, and you need to know how to take your time.

"Everyone stops to make tea here and there, and we also pull in at all the cafes, like the Lord Nelson Cheese Shop."

Yes, there is a cheese shop in Nelson, Wisconsin, though I don't recall that it was ever knighted.

"I believe Hilary and I could almost qualify to enter," I said. "Our Raleigh Capris are veritable antiques."

"Well, those old Raleigh's will last forever, but to participate your bike must have a three-speed hub." Tough luck.

We talked for a bit about Winnipeg—the several folk festivals, the new Museum for Human Rights, the historic riches in nearby St. Boniface, and the films of Guy Madden. I told them a friend and I once canoed from Lake Superior to Lake Winnipeg; they asked me what my route had been, I mentioned the English and the Wabagoon rivers, and that got them going on the Bloodvein River.

"When I was working for the Crown, we bought out the last remaining lodge on that river," he said. "The owners told us, 'Are you sure you want to see us go? We've saved a lot of lives over the years. We have the only phone for fifty miles.'"

Then we headed off for Frontenac State Park and our rendezvous with the orchard orioles.

It was a good day of birding, the tale of which I'll leave for another time. Road races entered the story again as we drove from Wykoff toward Forestville and came upon hundreds of bicyclists grinding out a long uphill stretch. There were more of them hanging around the Forestville State Park office, and yet more lounging in the yard in front of the historic barn at the far end of the now-closed bridge across the Root River.

Though most of the cyclists wore colorful lycra suits, many of which had club insignia, it was clear to me that this was not an ordinary race, either. There was lots of good feeling but not much urgency in the air.

We didn't find out what was going on until the next morning. Rain was imminent and we broke camp early, heading down to the picnic pavilion near the river to brew some coffee. A few minutes later a bedraggled cyclist wandered into the shed. He had a black Manfred Mann beard and insect-wrap goggles. The metal toe-clips on his shoes rang on the concrete as he walked.

"What's with all the cyclists?" I asked.

"It's the Almanzo Wilder bike race," he replied, in slow, measured phrases. "It's a hundred-mile road race, mostly on gravel. It started out small, with maybe thirty cyclists, a few years ago, but it's grown, and this year I think there were more than a thousand entries. What makes it different is that it's free, and no one wins. Everyone who finishes the route is awarded a Mason jar full of gravel. It's mostly a personal challenge and a nice day of camaraderie for the people who enter."

"Is Almanzo Wilder some famous cyclist?" I asked. Hilary hastened to inform me that Almanzo was Laura Ingalls Wilder's husband. The Wilders once lived in nearby Spring Valley, where the race starts and finishes.

"But I'm doing something different," the cyclist said. "I'm riding a 380-mile loop down to Prairie du Chien and back. It sounded like a good adventure."

"When did you start?" I asked him.

"Friday morning. I've got thirty miles to go."

(That's 175 miles a day on gravelly hills. Jesus!)

"Were you in the campground last night? Where did you sleep?" I asked.

"In a ditch. My knee was really bothering me and I was holding up my friends, so they gave me an extra emergency blanket and went on without me. The knee's better this morning."

"Do you want some coffee?" Hilary asked.

"Are you offering me some coffee? That would be *so* good," he replied.

"With milk?" I asked.

So we gave him a cup of piping hot coffee and some banana chips.

Meanwhile, another couple had wandered into the pavilion. He was a trout fisherman—tall, balding, gray mustache; she was heavy-set, with character; she could have won a bit part as a hobbit herbalist in *The Lord of the Rings*.

We got to talking about trout fishing, and soon he was reciting all the little rivers in Michigan's Upper Peninsula he'd fished. Like us, they come to Forestville every spring.

"I might reread Hemingway's "Big Two-Hearted River" when we get home tonight," I said.

"But he wasn't writing about *that* river," the man replied. "You can tell from the nearby towns he names."

"How has the fishing been here?" I asked. "I haven't seen many fishermen around. The water's awfully high...and muddy."

"Not good. Trout feed by sight, and they can't see much right now."

It was obvious that birds didn't interest him.

"There is one warbler that we always expect to see down here," I said. "We never see it anywhere else. The blue-winged warbler. It nests in the trees beyond Loop C. I heard one last night the moment we arrived at our campsite. But we haven't seen him yet."

I was going to do an imitation of the song—a faint sigh followed by a slobbery exhalation. But I knew it would have been pointless.

As we talked the air lightened. The fisherman's wife had built a fire in the fireplace the moment they arrived, using the method of building the little fire on top of the big logs rather than underneath it. The bicyclist had gone over to warm himself in front of it. By this time we'd poured him a second cup of coffee; he was still cradling the plastic cup in his hands.

At one point a bird shot through the open building and landed on a picnic table beyond.

"Did you see that?" the fisherman said.

"Female redstart," I said.

"He shot right through the pavilion," he said.

We eventually retrieved our cup from the cyclist, who was warming himself by the fire, and as we left I said, "Have a safe trip. It's an impressive feat you're undertaking. Maybe we'll see you again out on the road."

"Thanks," he said.

Then we went back to the campground to hunt up that blue-winged warbler.

Puffins Stuffed with Cake

M agnus Nilsson is an internationally renowned chef, thirty-two years old, whose restaurant, Fäviken, is currently ranked number nineteen on the San Pellegrino World's Best Restaurants list. The restaurant sits in the basement of a lodge on a remote island in the Baltic Sea 270 miles north of Stockholm. I suspect neither you nor I will be going there any time soon.

What we *could* do, not so long ago, was stop in at the American Swedish Institute in South Minneapolis to see some of the snapshots Magnus took of Icelandic landscapes, exotic sea birds, farmhouse interiors, men harvesting guillemot eggs on sea cliffs, and moss soup.

The photos came from Magnus's recently published book, *The Nordic Cookbook*. The show itself has been given the title Magnus Nilsson's Nordic: A Photographic Essay of Landscapes, Food and People, and when the images are blown up to six by ten feet, they're wonderful to behold.

Well, anyone with an iPhone could take spectacular photos of the Nordic countryside nowadays, and Magnus knows that. In one of the text panels he remarks that he has always enjoyed taking snapshots, and doesn't care much whether they're good or bad. It's just a record of what strikes him as interesting or beautiful at a given time.

The show was given added dimension, of course, by the connections with food and cooking. It conveyed a sense of rural simplicity combined with deep knowledge of local plants and animals, a "peasant" environment but with serious craftsmanship, historical patina, and sophisticated tastes. In viewing the photos, I felt I was once again entering the realm of fairy tales, although the payoff (as it were) came not at the conclusion to the story, when the frog turns into the prince, but in the majesty of the frog himself—or the wooden silo, the earthen baking pits, the caribou on the hillside, the eggs in the nest.

It was a stroke of genius to scatter wooden recipe boxes here and there throughout the exhibit. Each box contained multiple copies of three or four recipes, and each selection was different, so you could emerge from the show with ten or twelve recipe cards and save yourself the $50 cost of the book, though you'd miss out on the color photos and the text.

Right now I'm looking at a recipe for smoked eel and scrambled eggs. Here's one for moss soup that reminds me of my Boy Scout days. Then there's the one for Icelandic rye bread, and another for puffin stuffed with cake.

The back of each card contains additional cooking information along with historical lore. For example:

Puffins on the Faroe Islands are most often filled with a sort of cake batter mixed with raisins, sewn shut and braised, or just braised without the cake. The batter can also be wrapped in little pouches of aluminum foil and braised together with the birds rather than inside them. Leave the plucked, gutted and cleaned puffins to soak in cold water overnight before cooking them. They have a peculiar but tasty, fresh-ocean flavor to them, which can grow very strong and a bit heady for my taste if they are not handled well.

The exhibit was further bolstered by photos taken at Magnus's restaurant, a small display of wooden bowls and utensils made by Minnesota artisans, and a three-minute video of Magnus himself talking. He seemed like a down-to-earth guy, fun-loving, adventurous, and not terribly stuck on himself.

Although the photo of shark-meat smørrebrød near the end of the show was less than appetizing, we were neverthe-less keen on getting a snack of some kind at Fika, the Swed-ish Institute's pleasant café. In the end, however, we decided that there were too many things in the fridge back home that needed to be eaten soon, including some aging green beans and a clump of wilting dill. So we stopped at Lund's on our way home and picked up a few things to flesh out an early summer meal.

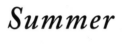

Summer

Summer Solstice Reading List

The news from Palomar Observatory is unequivocal. Yes, the days are now getting shorter again. Should we be sad?

For the last week I've been able to see a pink sky when going to bed and another pink sky the following morning before getting up. That's kind of cool.

Nowadays our "midsummer" festivities seldom go beyond some grilling on the deck with friends, an overnight to a nearby state park, and a bike ride or two. This year Hilary and I set up camp and walked the trails at Lake Carlos State Park, two hours northwest of the Cities, then unfolded our chairs on the park's deserted beach to watch the tree swallows jive and dart above the water in the waning light. While we were sitting there we spotted a group of women doing "cobra" and "downward-facing dog" on paddleboards out in the middle of the reedy lake.

Nature has outgrown its freshness, its youthful tenderness, its surprising loveliness, and now exhibits a fulsome vigor. The birds are still singing, but they're no longer showing themselves as often. Though various plants will bloom, each in its time, the scene won't change much for the next two months. Our mission—our duty!—is to get out into it.

When we're not out scouring the countryside (or inside

doing "real" work) I have also been doing some reading along these mid-summer lines, and I've come to the conclusion that Nature isn't that easy to write about convincingly. That is to say, reading about plants, animals, landscapes, and natural processes seldom generates the same kind of affection for one's surroundings that being out in them does. Maybe this is because Nature doesn't have a plot. It reaches us as a long succession of *amuse-bouches*, with a pleasant soundtrack humming quietly in the background.

As the recent pandemic forced us all to spend more time indoors, I found myself drawn more than ever to simple, earthy prose. Homespun descriptions of rural life offered a meager but effective counterweight to daily death tolls. I steered clear of the environmental harangues that are so common these days (important though they may be), and I also avoided narratives of wilderness adventure, which tend to focus on human endurance and close calls with disaster rather than the supple and harmonious interactions of living things.

It may seem that I'm isolating a narrow slice of experience here, but I had no trouble finding things to satisfy the need, from children's books (Selma Lagerlöf's *The Wonderful Adventures of Nils Holgersson*) to fiction (Jean Giono's *Blue Boy*) to reappraisals of agricultural history (James McGregor's *Back to the Garden: Nature and the Mediterranean World from Prehistory to the Present*) to memoir (Swedish entomologist Fredrik Sjoberg's brilliant and wide-ranging essay *The Fly Trap*.) But the book that offered perhaps the most satisfying read was Hal Borland's *Beyond Your Doorstep: A Handbook to the Country*.

Alfred Knopf published the book back in 1962, but I spotted a pristine copy of the first edition just last summer at Beagle and Wolf Books, a small but well-stocked shop in Park Rapids. The front endpaper carries an inscription: "Alice and Hamlet, from Plummer and Ida, Dec-25-1963," written with a fountain pen in elegant cursive script that resembles my mother's handwriting—and that of many other women of her time. Although by 1962 Knopf had been sold to Random House, the book is decorated with the same sort of wing-dings we find in earlier Knopf editions stretching from Sigurd Olson's canoeing essays back to the works of Wallace Stevens, Willa Cather, and Thomas Mann.

To judge from the lack of wear, I don't think Alice and Hamlet ever got around to reading the book. Borland describes it in the foreword as a handbook rather than a field guide. His goal is "to indicate what to look for and where and when." If he inspires the reader to move on to guide books for details, then Borland will consider his purpose to have been fulfilled.

Perhaps he was being modest, but such a précis fails to account for the intrinsic value—I'm tempted to say the "poetry"—of the prose itself, which draws on both the author's vast knowledge of the natural world and his relaxed, slightly folksy New England tone. Though he wrote regularly for the *New York Times*, Borland spent much of the year on his farm in northwestern Connecticut. And he makes it clear, early on, that he knows the names of the trees, the bugs, and the fish, how they interrelate, and where they're likely to be found. Excluding genuine wilderness from his purview, he focuses on phenomena that anyone in the eastern United States might easily come upon during a two-hour hike down a country road or fifteen minutes in a barn. To dip into any of the first six chapters, which range from "Pastures and Meadows" to

"The Bog and the Swamp" and "Flowing Waters," might be the next best thing to actually taking such a walk.

> *Come mid-April and the shadblow blooms in the riverside woods like tall spurts of shimmering white mist among the leafless trees. I first knew shadblow in the high mountains of southwestern Colorado, which simply proves how broad is the range of this cousin of the apple. But I knew it there as serviceberry. In the Northeast it gets the name shadblow or shadbush because it comes to blossom when the shad come up the streams to spawn—or did come when the streams were habitable for shad, not heavily polluted. It blossoms in tufts of small, white, long-petaled flowers before the leaves appear.*

As an aside, I might mention that the name "serviceberry" also has a New England derivation: The tree blooms in the spring at just the time when the ground has thawed enough to make it feasible to conduct burial services for those who had died the previous winter.

At a few points later in the book, Borland's attention veers off in less personal directions, as if his editor had told him, "Hal, you've got to write a chapter on the night sky. And how about one on foraging? And poisonous plants?" We don't need to be told that the five major planets are Mercury, Venus, Mars, Jupiter, and Saturn, for example. To his credit, in the section on foraging Borland describes quite a few edible plants, one after another, but doesn't shrink from admitting that most of them taste terrible and are not worth the effort required to gather them.

The chapter on birds also seems a little weak, though it runs to twenty-eight pages. Borland clearly knows his birds; he mentions that in the course of a given summer he is sometimes able to distinguish between five individual Baltimore orioles on the basis of slight variations in their song. But he spends less times sharing his encounters with the warblers, vireos, flycatchers, and raptors in the woods around his farm than assuring readers that birding isn't as hard as it may seem, and encouraging them to buy binoculars.

All the same, there are a few things to be learned or enjoyed on nearly every page of this welcoming and erudite ramble across the New England countryside. And near the end of the book, Borland draws upon all the lore he's been sharing to take us through a brief tour of the passing seasons, month by month. As a wrap-up, he devotes an entire chapter to the issue of common versus scientific names, and provides a long list of equivalents.

Shadblow? Serviceberry? We're talking here about the *Amalanchier canadensis*.

THERE'S A LOT TO BE said for those writers who divvy out tidbits of information to help us "understand" nature, but I don't take kindly to the "scientists have shown that" terminology that often accompanies these reports. I don't need a scientist to validate something I've already observed in the field many times. In any case, I prefer a more poetic approach, where the challenge lies in somehow avoiding generalities while making a few details stand for a larger whole.

I brought a thick book of Antonio Machado's poems out on the deck a few nights ago. It was the perfect book for the evening. For example:

> ... *the wind blows in squalls,*
> *and between clouds and clouds*
> *are patches of indigo sky.*

Water and sun. The rainbow gleams.
In a remote cloud
zigzags
a thread of yellow lightning.

The rain batters the window
and the panes chime.

In the midst of the haze
shaped by the fine drizzle,
a green meadow emerges
and an oak forest blurs
and a mountain ridge is lost...

Though nothing here is very specific, this sounds very much like experience to me. But having read one page, I'm likely to sit back and stare off into space with an inaudible but satisfied "hmmm" on my lips.

The other day I took a look at *Mute Objects of Expression* by the quasi-surrealist French poet Francis Ponge, known for his minute examinations of everyday objects. In the introductory pages of this squarish paperback Ponge espouses a radical devotion to whatever specific thing he chooses to describe, eschewing the limpid turns of poetic phrasing that might naturally come to mind.

From now on, [he writes] *may nothing ever cause me to go back on my resolve: never sacrifice the object of my study in order to enhance some verbal turn discovered on the sub-ject, nor piece together any such discoveries in a poem.*

Always go back to the object itself, to its raw quality, its difference: particularly its difference from what I've (just then) written about it.

May my work be one of continual rectification of

expression on behalf of the raw object (with no a priori concern about the form of that expression)...Recognize the greater right of the object, its inalienable right, in relation to any poem.

This approach raises some thorny epistemological questions, however. Does the poet, at any time, have a direct, objective, and unmediated awareness of his or her "object"? Can a description "capture" a thing faithfully, in the raw? I think not.

In the essay/poems that follow, Ponge takes up, describes, or inquires after a variety of "things," including a wasp, birds, a mimosa tree, and a carnation. He seems to be tussling with his own wayward imagination as he puts forth an adjective or a verbal phrase intended to convey some aspect of the creature or element under review, and as a result, the pieces often have a tone of playful nonsense.

Mimosa (prose poem). - A single spray of the hypersensitive golden chick plumes, seen through binoculars two kilometers down the lane, pervades the house. Full blown, the little mimosa balls give off a prodigious fragrance and then contract; they have lived. Are they flowers of the rostrum? Their speech, unanimously heeded and applauded by the throng with nostrils wide, carries far:

"MIraculous
MOmentary
SAtisfaction!

MInute
MOssy
SAffroned!"

Combs discouraged by the beauty of the golden lice born of their teeth! Lower yard upper yard of rooted ostriches,

erupting with golden chicks. Brief fortune, young million-
airess with dress fanned-out, tied at the base, fluttered in
bouquets ...

Within this play of free associations, the mimosa itself
returns to our attention repeatedly—presuming we already
know what a mimosa sprig looks like!

I kind of like it.

But I think some benevolent editor ought to change the
title of Ponge's collection: not *Mute Objects of Expression* but
Mute Objects of Affection.

Stopping to Smell the Lindens

In some vague and irrational way, I thought it was *my* fault when, year after year, the linden tree beside the driveway failed to produce that glorious fragrance for which it's famous. Did I cut back the low-hanging branches too recklessly? Did I neglect to fertilize? (But who fertilizes an eighty-foot tree?) The long green wings (which are called bracts, I think) appeared, yes. The little seeds dangling beneath, yes. But beyond that, nothing except a carpet of desiccated pods strewn across the driveway. I had dim recollections of a time when the tree smelled sweet. Something had gone terribly wrong.

And then, this year, everything went right. Perhaps it was the rain. Whatever the case may be, the tree fruited up handsomely and began to emit its wonderful scent.

Yet as I mentioned this phenomenon to friends, it soon became clear to me that the scent of the linden isn't so famous after all. Many of them had never noticed the smell, and often had no idea what a linden tree looks like.

In case you think I'm exaggerating the appeal of this delectable, if short-lived, summer phenomenon, here's a passage from *A Natural History of Trees* by Donald Culross Peattie, written in an age when rhapsodic prose was nothing to be ashamed of:

When the shade begins to be heavy and the midges fill the woods, and when the western sky is a curtain of black nimbus slashed by the jagged scimitar of lightning, when the wood thrush seldom sings except after rain and instead the rain crow, our American cuckoo, stutters his weary, descending song—an odor steals upon the moist and heavy air, unbelievably sweet and penetrating.

It is an odor that comes from no bed of stocks, no honeysuckle. More piercing, yet less drugging, than orange blossoms, it is wafted, sometimes as much as a mile, from the flowers of the Linden. All odors have evocative associations to those who know them well — wild grape, wild Crab, wild rose and honeysuckle. The odor of the Lindens in bloom brings back to many of us the soaring wail of the treetoads, the first fireflies in the dusk, the banging of June beetles on the window screens, the limpness of the flags at Fourth of July, and all that is a boy's-eye view of those languorous first days of vacation from school.

Reading further in Peattie's entry, I came upon a bit of trivia that I found reassuring: the linden produces its honey only two or three out of every five years. That goes a certain way toward explaining the intermittent and unpredictable behavior of our tree.

This afternoon Hilary and I swept the flowers, seeds, and bracts off the driveway. Many are still hanging on, so we'll have to do it again, but we'd just returned from a bike ride down to Loring Park followed by lunch at a neighborhood café in Bryn Mawr, and we felt like being outside. It didn't take long.

Unlike the rose, you don't have to "stop and smell" the linden. At its best, the aroma is pervasive. Most often, you smell it first, then look around for those pale green bracts and flowers hanging from the dark green heart-shaped leaves of a nearby tree.

In case you're interested, the sidewalk on the south side of Gold Medal Park, next to the Guthrie Theater in downtown Minneapolis, has been planted with a double row of lindens. There's usually a meter available on the east end of the park. Why not drive down this weekend, get an ice cream cone at Izzy's across the street, and take a stroll along that shady boulevard, and maybe even up the spiral trail to the top of the hill? You might catch a lingering whiff of this heavenly midsummer aroma. Then you'll recognize it the next time it comes floating by.

Russ the Arborist

An arborist stopped by this afternoon to give me an estimate on a few clean-up jobs on our suburban plot. I'd noticed that one of the volunteers growing near a corner of the house we seldom visit was dying. Yellow leaves were peeking over the rooftop. Russell took one glance over the shingles and said, "Looks like Dutch elm disease to me."

We wandered around to that side of the house to discover that there were two elms, side by side, in distress. That was news to me.

"These will have to go," he said. "When the city sees them they'll give you thirty days to remove them." That was an easy decision to make.

On our way back to the front yard I pointed out four trees that have sprouted along the side of the house and now reach above twenty feet in height.

"For a few years I thought these were sumac," I said. "Then I noticed they weren't suckering. Then it dawned on me—they're walnut trees! Do you think they're too close to the house?"

"I'd remove that one by the window well," Russell said. "Otherwise they look fine to me."

Back in the front yard, I did my best to point out a few

dead branches concealed within the now-verdant foliage of a forty-foot basswood tree. Then it was around to the back, where we examined the drooping branches of a large silver maple that were blocking garden sunlight and flirting with the power-lines running to the house.

"I would recommend cutting that entire branch off back to the trunk," Russell suggested. "We'll have to arrange with the power company to shut off the electricity. You might be out for the whole day."

"We lose power here three or four times a year anyway," I said. "It's because of all the trees."

"Often the other side of the street is fine. You see these thick cables running in and out of windows and across the street."

"Same thing in our neighborhood," he said.

Russell had an easy-going manner and an obvious enthusiasm for trees. It was like talking to Gary Snyder's little brother. We had long since entered a comfortable chatting zone, and having come to the end of my arboreal to-do list, I said, "See any other tree issues crying out for attention?"

"Things look good. You have a lot of nice trees. But this oak—" he said, pointing to a pin oak fifteen feet from the deck. "You see that dark vein in the leaf?"

"I know, it's an iron deficiency. It used to be worse."

"Iron and manganese. You probably have clay soil, which tends to be more acidic. We could inject the tree with an active agent that would be effective for three years. But it costs $250."

"I don't know," I said, "I sort of like that dark vein in the leaf. Ten years ago lots of the leaves were entirely yellow. And a tree just grows until it dies, anyway."

"That's true," Russell agreed. "Ninety percent of all trees die. They get out-competed."

I think he meant to say that ninety percent of all trees die before reaching maturity. (All trees die eventually.)

"What about these?" I asked, turning in the opposite direction toward three tall spruce trees standing in a row, bare trunks rising to considerable height before the tufts of needles commence. "In 1948 our former neighbor planted them as $1 seedlings. I suppose they might have to go eventually."

"That wouldn't be cheap. Difficult access, power lines right there. I would guess $6,000. But they're doing fine for now."

"They used to have needles down to the ground. But I've read that Colorado spruce can live to 600 years."

"That seems like a stretch. Certainly not in this environment. Sitka spruce on the West Coast might live that long," he said. Then he added, as if to cheer me up, "White pine can go to three hundred years or more."

"I've seen some old ones in the Boundary Waters. And the Lost Forty. But you know, they're not that much bigger than a hundred-year-old pine. And they're widely scattered. It's not like you're walking through Muir Woods or anything."

Turns out Russell had just gotten back from Muir Woods—a redwood grove on the California coast north of San Francisco. "That's my first time out that way," he said. "Awesome."

At that point our conversation turned to how little people know about trees. I mentioned that I once spent a week in Yosemite without meeting a single person who knew how to differentiate between the Jeffries pine from the ponderosa— even the rangers. I don't know either. Then it was on to old growth forests, pockets of virgin timber up near Lac La Croix that we'd both visited on Oyster and Gebeoniquet Lakes.

"When I was in high school I considered becoming a forester," I mentioned at one point. "I even attended a forestry camp called Trees for Tomorrow in Eagle River, Wisconsin. I'm not sure how I ended up in European history."

Eventually I went back inside and Russell wandered the yard with his clipboard, then sat in his car for half an hour writing up a proposal, drawing a map and numbering all the trees in the yard backward from ninety-nine.

The final proposal didn't look too bad to me. Two thirds of it—removing the elms—was required by law.

"Should I sign this?" I asked.

"If you feel it's necessary."

"Doesn't matter to me."

So we set up a tentative date-range, dependent on getting the power company out to turn off the electricity.

And then he was telling me about the Midway-Frogtown Arborators Band, for which he plays the saxophone. They're doing a gig at the Turf Club next week.

Minneapolis Walkabout

What a day! Cool and clear, after the thunderstorm in the night that got me up to unplug the computer.

Household projects ditched, we oil our chains, inflate our tires, and are off around the lakes. Orioles chirp from the cottonwoods, with vireos warbling from the lower story. Cool wind off the lakes, I veer left toward the muddy paths along Dean Parkway, forgetting the normal route along the Midtown Greenway.

At Harriet we wander the rock garden, admiring the wildflowers. The blooms in the perennial garden across the road are more colorful and robust, but perhaps no more interesting. Swinging north past the bandshell, we come upon a mass of school children surrounding the stage. We'd seen them earlier in smaller groups, walking along the footpath with teachers and chaperones, happy to be out of the classroom. It seems they're handing out awards for Clara Barton School. One young man broke his own school record for pull-ups. Last year twenty-one, this year twenty-three.

We cut across some parking lots at the north end of Lake Calhoun and find ourselves in front of Rustica Bakery. Naturally, we stop in for a baguette and a couple of cookies. Riding back through the woods along the rail-lines to the car, I check my shadow from time to time to make sure the bread's still back there. We're stopped by a train south of Cedar Lake—it picks up steam as it heads into the city.

Lunch across town at Gandhi Mahal on Minnehaha and Lake. This is an interesting intersection, what with Mosaic (great Bánh mì meatloaf sandwich), Midori's Floating World (Japanese), Patrick's Caberet, a back-alley flamenco workshop, El Nuevo Rodeo, and the Harriet Brewery all in close proximity. I never met an Indian restaurant I didn't like—Delights of India, Star of Indian, Taste of India, Dancing Ganesha—but maybe the buffet at Gandhi Mahal is a cut above. The mango lassi is also good. And a genuine atmosphere of "peace" prevails.

Overstuffed, we head south along leafy Minnehaha Avenue in search of Moon Palace Books. There it is! Nestled behind Trylon Microtheater and Peace Coffee. A young man is sitting on the pavement outside the shop wrestling with an inky-looking bale of hay encased in an airy crate. He explains that they've been grooming the hay to support the flowers they're going plant to brighten up the boulevard.

Inside, we chat with the friendly, self-confident proprietress named Angela about Halldór Laxness and Edith Perlman as we peruse the shop's small but well-chosen stock. She looks vaguely familiar, but I can't place her.

"Are you from the neighborhood?" she asks at one point.

"Pretty close…Golden Valley."

Yes, a good selection of books. In the end, I actually buy one! *Notes of the Possibilities and Attractions of Existence: Selected Poems of Anselm Hollo.*

Back in the car with Hilary and Anselm, puttering across South Minneapolis, I say, "Read one. Just read a short one."

THE IMAGE OF DAY RECEDES

The pleasure principle tends to start sqeaking after a while
just like this wood frame canvas chair of mine
does to remind me that nothing related to human
activity is simply automatic, or predictably continuous

"How about one more?" I ask.

The laundry basket lid is still there though badly chewed
up by the cat but time has devoured the cat entirely.

On our way to the Minneapolis Institute of Arts we stop at Electric Fetus. It's not only a record store but an institution. No, I'm not going to buy an antiwar poster or some incense or a hipster cap any time soon. But the Fetus is still the head shop and music mecca par excellence that it was back in the 1970s, when we biked over from the University, asking ourselves, "Why did they put it here?"

Nor has the neighborhood been gentrified much in the course of the decades. Franklin Avenue has a few more bakeries and clinics than it used to, but it's as gritty as ever.

Of course, music downloading, and now streaming, has taken its toll on the Fetus. I had heard that the jazz section was sorely depleted but find that it isn't as bad as I'd feared. I hang on to a compilation of three early Ornette Coleman LPs for quite a while as I wander the aisles, but in the end decide to take the plunge on new and local material: *Excelsior*, Bill Caruthers, solo piano.

Our visit to the Art Institute, which is right around the corner from the Fetus, is further delayed by a detour up to 27th Street to see if our friends Dana and Mary are home. As we drive by I honk at a woman with hair blowing wild in the wind who's wandering down the sidewalk. It's Mary!

"Hi!" she says. "I was just going next door to see when the new clinic is going to open. This used to be an Ethiopian coffee shop. The sign on the door says it will open tomorrow. Huh? Written with a ball-point pen. Not very professional, do you think?"

Mary gives us a tour of their gardens—they hacked down the clematis this spring. Dana emerges from the "office" upstairs and we sit on the porch watching the world go by.

The show at the Institute, Art in an Age of Truthiness, sounded a little odd, but it proved to be well worth a visit. We entered via the grandiose "old" doorway, up the long flight of steps facing the park. I love going in that way. You're already on the second floor, only a few steps from the featured exhibits. They were getting ready for a gala dinner, setting places and taping heavy wires to the floor between the tables.

The show itself? It was cool, diverse, trivial, mesmerizing. The premise itself is flawed, in so far as art is never "true," strictly speaking, but quite a few of the installations were fascinating. I liked the Freudian Coney Island artifacts, whether real or fake; the photos of passing outer-space objects; the digital collage nature canvases of Joel Lederer, which are no different from any other landscape in conception; and the branding doll anime avatar (I don't remember her name) who was given her freedom and vanished, leaving behind a three-minute farewell note. The best, however, was a luscious big-screen reenactment of what the characters who appear in "Las Meninas" were doing immediately before and after the scene Velázquez depicted on canvas.

The Second Half of the Year

It has been my experience that the second half of the year is often better than the first half. We're talking mid-summer, with the state fair on the horizon. Then glorious September.

Better how? Maybe it's just the satisfaction of knowing that so many warm months lie ahead, and when the darkness does start to close in, there will be plenty of gatherings and musical events to distract us. But that seems too analytical. I think it has more to do with the burden of the months lifting. In any case, the summer months breed confidence, as if we've completed a climb, exhilarating but peppered with hardship, and it's all downhill from here.

Hardship? This isn't something I think about a whole lot, even in springtime. A little trouble with the knee as the result of some reckless moves on the tennis court. A night in a tent under six hours of thunder and quite a bit of rain.

One pleasant challenge that I face in late spring every year is to make thoughtful use of the cash I receive from Hilary's parents as a birthday gift, which they encourage me to spend on something fun or unusual, knowing full well that they don't need to twist my arm very hard. This wad of cash loosens up my approach to the Daedalus summer remainder catalog, among other things.

This year I placed the following order:

– A six-CD set of the Beaux Art Trio playing Mozart's complete piano trios
   – *The Event of Literature* by Terry Eagleton
   – *An Englishman in Madrid* by Eduardo Mendoza
   – *Dante in Love* by A. N. Wilson

At an art fair in St. Anthony Park I happened upon another golden opportunity, landing 10 jazz CDs at $1 per disc. Among the highlights were:

   – Cassandra Wilson: *Standards*
   – Fred Hersch: *Solo Monk*
   – Nicolas Payton: *Gumbo Nouveau*
   – *The Ultimate Bill Evans*
   – Charlie Haden/ Hank Jones: *Steal Away—Spirituals, Hymns and Folk Songs*
   – Steve Lacy/ Roswell Rudd: *Monk's Dream*

The one book I purchased at that event was the Phillip Lopate's anthology, *The Art of the Personal Essay*. I cracked it open a few days later and was charmed by Max Beerbohm, whom I had previously known only through an unflattering cartoon. Near the end of one essay Beerbohm drops the thread of his story to reflect on how weak his recollections are:

It is odd how little remains to a man of his own past— how few minutes of even his memorable hours are not clean forgotten, and how few seconds in any one of those minutes can be recaptured... I am middle-aged, and have lived a vast number of seconds. Subtract ? of these, for one mustn't count sleep as life. The residual number is still enormous. Not a single one of those seconds was unimportant to me in its passage. Many of them bored me, of course; but even boredom is a positive state: one chafes at it and hates it; strange that one should afterwards forget it! And stranger still that of one's actual happinesses and unhappinesses so tiny and tattered a remnant clings about one!

Memories do tend tò fade, recombine, blend together, and rearrange themselves into more convenient narrative structures. Maintaining an accurate chronology is simply not in the cards. Earlier this morning I booked a campsite at Crow Wing State Park. Hunting around for some photos of our last visit, which seems like a distant memory, I was surprised to discover it was only a year ago—almost to the day. Beerbohm makes a similar point.

Memory is a great artist, we are told; she selects and rejects and shapes and so on. No doubt. Elderly persons would be utterly intolerable if they remembered everything. Everything, nevertheless, is just what they themselves would like to remember, and just what they would like to tell to everybody. Be sure that the Ancient Mariner, though he remembered quite as much as his audience wanted to hear, and rather more, about the albatross and the ghastly crew, was inwardly raging at the sketchiness of his own mind.

What will I remember of the spring just past? The summer tanager we saw out at the arboretum, five hundred miles north of his normal range? The bright morning tourist cruise around Duluth Harbor? The gritty flamenco show we saw at the Ice House? The get-together on the deck with friends? The bike ride through the woods to Utepils, our own local brew pub, on a glorious weekday afternoon?

I drove down to the Antiquarian Bookfair this morning.

(Come to think of it, I did that a year ago, too.) On my visit today I ran into a few old friends and chatted with a woman who's looking for someone to write a book about a sculptor she knows, recently deceased. (I gave her my card.)

I was not moved to buy anything, but I stopped by our local library on the way home to pick up a request that had come in and spotted two possible gems in the Friends of the Library booksale cart by the front door: *The Conscience of the Eye: the Design and Social Life of Cities* by Richard Sennett and *The Darkening Glass: a Portrait of Ruskin's Genius* by John Rosenberg.

There are blue jays everywhere these days, squawking and reeling. Mostly it's the young ones, I think, enjoying their newfound wings. Summer is just getting started. The afternoon sunlight is sublime. An atmosphere of unfocus descends, sweet and strangely passive, and it's hard to say when I'll get cracking on any of these books. Yet dipping into the book on Ruskin, I come almost immediately upon this passage: "Ruskin was eye-driven, even photoerotic, and confessed to 'a sensual faculty of pleasure in sight'...[He] looked at the material universe with preternatural vivacity and clarity, and believed that what he saw was divine."

Come Up to the Lab

The laboratory is nestled on the right bank of the Mississippi River, ensconced beyond the gray metal cages of a battery of Excel Energy transformers. The signs at the driveway leading down to it say Private Property, Keep Out. It's much easier to spot from the opposite side of the river—a boxy four-story building with banners hanging off it: EARTH WATER LIFE in a slightly rounded san serif font that's long been popular in the scientific community. Someone with good eyesight or binoculars might make out the sign adjacent: SAFL Outdoor Stream Lab.

I was delighted recently to receive an invitation from the U of M's alumni association to tour the lab.

I was one of perhaps fifty-thousand to whom the email was addressed, but I expressed an interest, and Hilary and I were given a slot on a one-hour afternoon tour. It turned out to be a two-hour tour, but I'm not complaining. There's a lot going on down there in the lab.

There may have been twelve of us in the group. Communications director Barbara Heitkamp started us off with a twenty-minute Powerpoint presentation. "I usually don't do this," she said, "but we're not going to be able to see the bottom floor of the lab, because we might disturb the fish in one of our experiments, so I thought I'd use the extra time to give you all an overview of what we're currently working on."

This turned out the be a blessing in disguise, because the visuals Barbara projected onto the screen gave a more vivid impression of some of the experiments than merely looking at wave machines and wind tunnels possibly could. For example, she showed us a video clip of snowflakes illuminated by floodlights as they whiz past a big wind turbine at night out in a field in Rosemount. You could see the eddies forming consistently in some places and the relative speed of the wind at various heights.

She also gave us a brief history of the building, which was built in the 1930s and has been used as a hydraulics lab ever since.

Eventually we headed upstairs to take a look at the gigantic U-shaped wind tunnel, in which they were studying various aspects of wind power, including not only efficiency but issues related to noise pollution. They had discovered that the low rumble given off by the turbines—too low to be audible—makes some people seasick.

I was surprised to learn that in many experiments the substance they blow through the tunnel is a fine mist of olive oil. I suggested that if they grew enough lettuce on the grounds outside, they could put a big bowl of it at the end of the tunnel, catch the oil, and have salad for lunch every day.

I also had the temerity, when Barbara was done describing the tunnel and its uses, to ask where the wind actually came from. A big fan?

"Yes. It's right over there. We call it the 'BAF'—big-ass fan." Yes, but probably not when giving presentations to the Board of Regents.

From there it was two flights down to the floors below

the level of the Mississippi upstream from the nearby falls, with a brief stop first in some labs where they're investigating the growth of blue-green algae.

Down below the upstream water table, access to water flow was as easy as opening a spigot or a gate. Yet several of the experiments were very small in scale, and I had my doubts about whether anything of substance was being unearthed. On the one hand, a fancy laser had been installed that rode back and forth on a stainless steel track above the room. If I remember correctly, it was capable of registering 800,000 pieces of data in five seconds. Sounds like overkill to me. On the other hand, once a big delta had developed in a tank over the course of days or weeks of particle deposition, the common practice was to slice it in two, spray a long piece of white paper with adhesive, and press the paper against the now-exposed side of the deposits to capture the stratification. Rather low-tech, don't you think?

At one of the water tanks we observed an enthusiastic undergrad from St. Thomas who was creating a delta with very fine sand, a big pile of which was lying on the floor beside his desk. The goal was to track the patterns of deposit, so that it would become easier to identify the layers of minute hydrocarbon particles that might develop in "real life."

The entire enterprise reminded me of the summer I spent doing experiments at the bio-engineering lab on the main campus of the U. I was in charge of a machine designed to filter red blood cells from blood, allowing the plasma to flow in a continuous stream, thus obviating the need for cumbersome centrifugal separation. The machine didn't work; the blood cells popped open as they hit the filter, thus ruining the plasma. My job was to figure out the optimum pressure to avoid the hemolysis.

I don't need to go into the details of my research or the chain of events that turned my attention away from science toward history and literature, but the atmosphere in the lab was the same: jerry-rigged, one-of-a-kind machinery and bags of dog blood side by side with sophisticated viscometers and spectrophotometers. Graph paper, duct tape, and tin foil scattered here and there. In those days there were no computer screens.

The operations at the lab also reminded me of my brother's sixth-grade science project—a plywood water tray the size of a small surfboard covered with metal filings, over which water flowed continuously. As you set obstacles of varying dimensions into the flow, the patterns in the filings would shift. It was fun to play with.

I was also reminded of how memorable those childhood days are when heavy rain sends water gushing alongside curbs and through gullies. There were plenty of undeveloped areas in the neighborhood where I grew up, and as freshets poured through the woods and fields and roads it was mesmerizing to toss a twig of just the right size and weight into the water and follow it as it floated downstream, bobbing past miniature rapids and plunging over waterfalls.

At our last stop we came upon three individuals—they might have been scientists or engineers but they looked like Mack and Meyer—fiddling with an antique motor rigged to a piston that generated waves by pushing a piece of plywood back and forth in a Plexiglas trough filled with green water. This contraption was being designed to study the morphology of sediments deposited on a beach over time.

One of the men, whom Barbara introduced to us as Benjamin Erickson, turned out to be the building manager. Once again, he reminded me of people I used to work with at the bio-engineering lab—Gordie Voss, Dick Forstrum, Frank Dormand. I would characterize such people as brilliant children who had somehow worked their fascinating boyhood hobbies into lifelong careers, thus preserving their sense of wonder.

The guy told Barbara that we were in luck. The fish had been removed from the experimental tubes through which they were trying to swim and the lower floor was now open. We headed down another flight of stairs, and at the bottom we came upon a variety of experiments, and also relics of other experiments. One dated back to the Cold War era, and involved a joint study by Honeywell and the U.S. Navy of the fluid dynamics involved in shooting a missile from a submarine. The gigantic tubes used in this study stood next to an exposed limestone wall that was actually part of the riverbank. Nearby were some very large tanks that had originally been used to store the water supply for the city of St. Anthony until a cholera outbreak in the 1860s (if I remember correctly) underscored the need for a better system.

We reemerged into daylight above an outdoor stream bed that was being used to study the factors that keep mussel environments healthy. Every mussel in the stream had been fitted with a sensor that registered whether it was open or closed, twenty-four hours a day.

If everything works out as planned, soon we'll all be eating fresh mussels daily, covered in a fine mist of olive oil and salt extracted from the soil under a wind turbine. We'll be reading Herodotus and wondering why everyone was so anxious back in the twentieth century.

Shooting the Breeze

I call it an idle afternoon, though I knew I ought to be doing something productive. It was a beautiful day, the sky was clear, the air was very cool. I'd gotten up early, and the thought suddenly popped into my head—pesto time. Not the time to eat it, but to make it. This would entail a trip to the downtown farmer's market, a mere twelve minutes away, to pick up a few big clumps of fresh basil. Well, Friday is a very good time to visit. You can park right next to the stalls and crowds are non-existent, though quite a few vendors are there.

I left the house at 7:55, made a brief stop at the bridge over Bassett Creek to measure the water clarity, and continued down Plymouth Avenue to the delicate piano sounds of Emmanuel Chambrier. It occurred to me, as I drifted past Homewood Studios, that Chambrier has touches of Poulenc's zip, Satie's dream-like atmosphere, and Ravel's classic structure. He ought to be included among that stellar group of younger composers: the Godfather of Les Six.

Weaving my way into the parking lot between a Metro Mobility driver who was helping a passenger disembark and a fork-lift driver unloading a pallet of potatoes, I pulled into a spot alongside the flower stall that's been occupied by the same cheerfully spacey merchant for as long as I can remember.

As I climbed the concrete steps to the middle aisle I looked up and found myself face to face with some of the most attractive bundles of basil I'd ever seen, bright green and glistening, no doubt from a recent spray of water. Though I usually wander a bit, evaluating the various products, I didn't hesitate to purchase three bundles for $1 apiece.

All would have been well, had I not lingered, coming upon some nice eggplants and a carton of red onions. I love red onions in salads, but do we really need five of them? Then there were the sweet potatoes.

I made the pesto later that day, spooned it into ziplock bags, and tossed them into the freezer. We took care of the eggplant over the weekend by breading and baking them, then topping them with a tomato sauce that made use of some yellow onions. (Another purchase that I neglected to mention.)

So here I sit, wolfing down the remains of a quinoa salad from CostCo while thumbing through Thoreau's journals. It's his 200th birthday, more or less. We are sometimes given the impression that Thoreau was a woodsy loner who looked upon hardworking farmers as deluded materialists, but in fact he took a interest in all aspects of village and country life, and had a healthy respect for anyone who attended carefully to nature's ways whether wild or domestic. On February 22, 1852, he wrote:

> *After having read various books on various subjects for some months, I take up a report on Farms by a committee of Middlesex Husbandmen, and read of the number of acres of bog that some farmer has redeemed, and the number of rods of stone wall that he has built, and the number of tons of hay he now cuts, or of bushels of corn or potatoes he raises there, and I feel as if I had got my foot down on to*

the solid and sunny earth, the basis of all philosophy, and poetry, and religion even. I have faith that the man who redeemed some acres of land the past summer redeemed also some parts of his character. I shall not expect to find him ever in the almshouse or the prison. He is, in fact, so far on his way to heaven. When he took the farm there was not a grafted tree on it, and now he realizes something handsome from the sale of fruit. These, in the absence of other facts, are evidence of a certain moral worth.

The beauty of Thoreau's *Journal* is that you can dip in anywhere and are likely to find thoughts of poetic or philosophical interest, well expressed but not diluted by the desire to embroider or inflate to a loftier level.

If I were taking ten books to a desert island, the *Journal* would be one of them. I'm grateful that New York Review of Books has issued a splendid paperback edition, edited by Damion Searls, that runs to a mere 667 pages. I doubt if it contains a tenth of the original, but it will do me for a lifetime.

Bastille Day on a Bicycle

Bastille Day is the best holiday of the year—sort of. It comes in the middle of summer, unlike Midsommers Eve and other such holidays, and demands nothing beyond a celebration of freedom, pleasure, and fellow-feeling. It's like everyone having their birthday at the same time, without the onus of finding appropriate gifts or being in the limelight all alone.

Though the holiday is French in origin, it has long since taken on universalist connotations. No one today (outside of France, anyway) associates it with the storming of the Bastille in 1789—a dreadful event that ended with an angry mob decapitating some poor souls who were defending a worthless and largely unoccupied fortress prison in the middle of Paris. Bastille Day is a day, not for guillotines, but for accordions, the instrument of gayety, of the streets— the instrument of the people. It's also a day for eating and drinking. Part of the beauty is that Bastille Day has no form, no real traditions, no protocol. Yet it rises above mere hedonism through its emphasis on the right of all women and men to enjoy themselves publicly, *en masse,* from time to time.

We are reminded daily by current events in Egypt, Russia, and elsewhere, that many people don't actually possess such rights. Yet Bastille Day (at least outside of France) is not a day for issuing demands, beyond those of "Garçon, another glass of Chablis!" or "Let's dance."

Some Americans also seize upon Bastille Day as a celebration of the European sources of our arts, mores, and traditions. The ideas that went into the making of the American republic are largely European, of course, as are the languages we speak. The dialectic between American and European values and ideas is a source of unending fertility, intermittent and sometime acrimonious though it may be. From Benjamin Franklin to Alexis de Tocqueville, from Henry James to Jean-François Revel, from Thomas Jefferson to Jean Baudrillard, the transatlantic scrutiny is never ending.

But on Bastille Day we probably won't be reading such reflections, which don't go well with croissants and orange marmalade. Better, perhaps, a few lines from the Breton poet Eugène Guillevic:

Prenez un toit de vieilles tuiles
Un peu après midi.

Placez tout à côté
Un tilleul déjà grand
Remué par le vent,

Mettez au-dessus d'eux
Un ciel de bleu, lavé
Par des nuages blancs.
Laissez-les faire.
Regardez-les.

Denise Levertov translates this as:

Take a roof of old tiles
A short while after midday.

Place nearby
A fullgrown linden
Stirred by the wind.

Above them put
A blue sky washed
By white clouds.
Let them be.
Watch them.

You may be wondering what's become of the freedom, pleasure, and joyous fellow-feeling I spoke about a moment ago. Give it time, give it time.

Michel Foucault once remarked to Bernard Henri-Lévy that the question "Is the revolution possible?" had given way to a different and perhaps more troubling one: "Is the revolution desirable?" To which the answer, according to Henri-Lévy, a committed Leftist, was a clear "No."

What does this mean? It doesn't matter. On Bastille Day, such interchanges are no more (or less) amusing than an Edith Piaf tune.

I got an email one Bastille Day morning from the New York Review of Books touting their collection of French language reprints, and offering selected volumes at forty percent off. It was an interesting mix. There was Jean Giono's *Hill*. But reading the descriptive notes convinced me that it's the same novel that was originally called, in English, *Hill of Destiny*. I have the first American edition, published in 1928, right here on the shelf.

The film-maker Jean Renoir's book about his father, titled simply *Renoir, My Father*, is rich in that combination of casual rural charm and aesthetic sophistication which is the crowning achievement of early twentieth century French culture. However, I happen to have a copy right here on the shelf beside me, and also a book club edition—my "reader's copy," as it were—ready and waiting in the basement.

My French is as shaky as ever, but I'm pretty sure the third of the books on sale, Maupassant's *Like Death*, is a translation of *Fort Comme la Mort*, which I read just out of college, probably because Ford Madox Ford drew heavily on it for the plot of his early masterpiece *The Good Soldier*. I found a copy of *Fort Comme la Mort* at a musty used book store in a dreary part of Duluth a few blocks up the hill from Michigan Street, a neighborhood of churches and tenements, as part of a multi-volume set with cheap purple binding—a dollar per book. I'm quite sure this new translation, by Richard Howard, is far better. Tempting.

Then we have Henri de Montherland's *Chaos and Night*, which I read in the 1990s. All I remember is that it's the story of a cranky man and his daughter, exiled to Spain, following the bullfights and grumbling about the government. Were they Spanish or French? I don't recall. I liked its excoriating bitterness at the time. But do I want to re-read it?

The list moves on the Patrick Modiano, who won the Nobel Prize as recently as 2014. I read one of his books a few months ago. It seemed like a Simenon mystery, but without Inspector Maigret or the mystery. Maybe I ought to give him another chance.

ONE OF THE BEST WAYS to celebrate freedom, diversity, spontaneity, and fellow-feeling, is on a bicycle. Entirely without premeditation, Hilary and I began one recent Bastille weekend on a Friday morning with a bike trip downtown along the North Cedar Trail. The Walker Sculpture Garden made for a fitting urban pre-Bastille Day stop. The south end of the garden retains the grassy swards, crushed limestone walkways, rectangular layout, and old-fashioned humanist sculptures, that remind me of, yes, Paris. The north end has been replanted with prairie forbs and grasses, and on a blazing Friday morning it reminded me of rural South Dakota.

On Saturday we found ourselves, appropriately enough, standing at 8 a.m. in front of the one-time home of Pierre Bottineau, one of Minnesota's founding fathers. Sometimes referred to as the last of the mountain men, Bottineau was a Métis—half French, the other half an Ojibwe/Dakota mix. He founded Maple Grove and Red Lake Falls, once owned a big chunk of property along what is now Robert Street in downtown St. Paul, and developed a reputation during his lifetime as a skilled, sober-minded, fearless, and utterly reliable leader and guide. We made a mental note to return sometime to learn more about Bottineau when the house was open, and then proceeded along the lush, hilly asphalt trails of Elm Creek Regional Park.

Later that afternoon I put a few select CDs in the changer as we were making dinner: Gilles Chabenat's long set of hurdy-gurdy recording, enlivened by a few female vocals, and Nicolas Peyton's *Dear Louis*, a big band homage to Louis Armstrong and the spirit of New Orleans. We were following a recipe for a lamb tagine I copied from a *New York Times* article featuring quintessential Bastille Day recipes. The spices smelled good the minute they hit the pan—ginger, cinnamon, nutmeg. But I had failed to read the recipe to the point where it says: "Cook in the oven at 325 degrees for 2½ hours."

We hurried it along on the stove top, and the result was rich and tasty, though in the midst of all that flavor I couldn't tell the difference between the apricots and the meat.

Monday morning, feeling the need to extend Le Weekend in the French manner, we drove out to the community beach in Wayzata, on the shores of Lake Minnetonka, to ride the rail trails once again, this time to Mound and back. Afternoon thunderstorms had been forecast, and the west wind, coming in across the lake, was already filling our nostrils with the aroma of seaweed and dead fish. The ride itself was more pleasant than I'd remembered it, perhaps because it was cool at 8 a.m. and the weekend crowds were nowhere to be seen. During some stretches I felt like I was riding through the pages of *Better Homes and Gardens*, not the least bit envious, mind you, simply appreciative of the architecture and the landscaping.

Only a few thousand affluent people can enjoy living on this wonderful—if over-crowded—lake, but anyone with a bicycle can enjoy riding alongside it for an hour or two. That's the nature of the community-spirited, post-Bastille Day world we live in. Later, sitting with a latte on a bench in downtown Wayzata alongside stock-brokers and yoga instructors, we enjoyed the breeze and cringed at the deafening whistle of a passing train.

But now the thunderheads are arriving. Rumbling from every direction over the purr of the air conditioner. A glass of cheap white Burgundy in hand—although no genuine Burgundy, even the most generic, is all that cheap. I would turn off the computer and unplug it, just in case lightning strikes, but it's getting old, and I'm afraid it might never come on again.

Eclipse Fever

It all started in February, with a morning email from our friend Gayle: "There's going to be a total eclipse crossing the U.S. in August. Wanna go?"

By the end of the day, everyone she'd notified had come on board, and Gayle had reserved the "family" room at the Rocket Motel in Custer, South Dakota. This would be our springboard to the open skies of western Nebraska, across which the zone of eclipse totality lay.

The small group of friends who made up the ensemble have travelled together in various permutations since the 1970s. We'd been to the bottom of the Grand Canyon together, and we'd been to the bottom of Dark Canyon, Utah, together. On our first trip to the Boundary Waters, Tim and Carol had been expecting their first child; that child recently gave birth to *her* fourth child. We'd been to summer cabins on the North Shore, where we once spotted a Hudsonian curlew wandering along the roadside, and established the Curlew Club in honor of the occasion. More recently we've been to winter cabins north of Grand Rapids together, though the allure of cross-country skiing seems to be fading for some of us. One or two things had changed over the years, but here we were again, heading out on a cross-country adventure together.

Thirty years ago, we might all have clambered into a single car. This time, we took two. Thirty years ago, we might have planned a few meals and bought groceries. This time, we decided to wing it.

A few days after the initial proposal was bruited, I suggested that we take an extra day going out to make the nine-hour drive less onerous and give us time to explore the Badlands and the Black Hills a little. The notion met with approval and I booked two of the four remaining campsites in the Cedar Pass Campground.

At some point it dawned on me that we might need somewhere to stay *after* the eclipse and I booked a campsite at Chadron State Park, forty miles north of Alliance, Nebraska, the locale where we'd decided to view the big event.

As the big day approached, the hype surrounding the event intensified. Half a million people would be coming to Nebraska, we were told. The governor would be flying in to Alliance from Lincoln to give a speech at Carhenge, a few miles outside of town. I began to envision highways clogged with tourists and state highway patrol officers combing the back roads to ticket or incarcerate tourists who had simply pulled onto the shoulder to view the eclipse.

The town of Alliance had been planning for the event for two years, and they'd developed a website to describe all the activities planned in association with it: food trucks, rock-and-roll bands, games, educational events. We didn't care about any of that stuff. But when you're six-hundred miles away, it's hard to imagine how big the town really is or how many people will show up. In short, we didn't know quite what kind of a mess we were getting ourselves into, and imagination runs rampant.

The Alliance website identified no less than forty-six camping or viewing sites in the vicinity. I called up one near town, but he wanted $50 for a parking spot. I called another one who wanted only $10, but he didn't have porta-potties and could only take people with trailers. Then I called Sugar Farms, three miles north and east of town. The woman who answered the phone, Lexi, wanted $20 for the privilege of parking in her pasture. She took my name and said, "Just pay me when you get here." Fair enough.

THE BADLANDS

We got to the Badlands after a full day of driving. Having crossed the Missouri River, we were now in "the West": harsh, largely empty terrain, the land of coyotes and golden eagles, buffalo and pronghorn, sage brush and wide open spaces. There are badlands scattered here and there throughout the west, of course—heavily eroded but often graceful landforms with colorful strata and (sometimes) sharp peaks—but the Badlands of South Dakota deserve their capital B. Dry and forbidding in the noonday sun, they're often gorgeous when clothed in the glancing light and deep shadows of sunrise or sunset.

The campground had nary a shrub or tree for privacy, but it did have picnic tables and slabwood ramadas for shade. With the flanks of the Badlands rising a few hundred yards to the north of us, it struck me as great.

Our only near neighbor was a family of four from Seattle who were set up across the road. I met them by chance as I was wandering around, oblivious to my surroundings, trying to determine if the bird on a nearby post was a mountain bluebird or a western bluebird. Lowering my binoculars, I noticed I was standing in their campsite.

"Oh, pardon me," I apologized. "Do you know birds? I think that's a mountain bluebird. We don't have them in Minnesota."

"We don't have them in Washington, either," the man replied, with a bemused grin on his face.

He was a research biologist. He and his family had come out to see the countryside and also the eclipse. They were planning to intercept the historic event near Casper, Wyoming, on their way home. I promised him we would be quiet. "I hate noise in the campground," I said, as if to convince him of our benign intentions.

And we didn't make much noise that night. The wind was coming in so strong from the west, it often rose above the voices and the banging pots and pans. It was too warm to have a fire, but we ended up singing a few cowboy songs—"I Ride an Old Paint" and "Singin' His Cattle Call" among others—as the box wine continued to flow. We heard coyotes twice, high-pitched but distant, over the fluffle of the wind on the tents.

As night descended, the landscape had the feel of a gypsy camp, with individual couples and families minding their own business as they cooked, ate, chatted, headed off to the toilet building or the evening lecture at the amphitheater a quarter-mile away, or got ready for bed. One after another, the light from lanterns and hi-tech flashlights punctuated the darkness.

The wind blew for most of the night. The rainfly, just outside our tent but roughly a foot from my ear, went wuff-wuff-wuff incessantly, but at irregular intervals, seemingly forever. I might have woken up twenty times before dawn, but they all seemed like the same time, so the damage was minimal.

The next morning Tim told me their tent, quite tall but lacking the support of rainfly guywires, sometimes bent over so much that it was flat to the ground with the three of them inside it. Yet the poles didn't snap, and a few seconds after such an event the tent would bound up again like one of those stove-pipe man-balloons you see on the roadside in front of a car dealership.

We ate breakfast at the restaurant of the nearby Cedar Pass Lodge. Hilary had spotted a sign on the door on our way in, advertising a buffalo butchering that we could attend at ten that morning. I asked our waitress if she was Oglala. "Yes, I'm from Kyle," she replied.

"Are you going to go to the buffalo butchering this morning?" I said. (Stupid question. But it gets the conversation going.)

"No, I'll be working," she replied, "but a few weeks ago my parents were given the honor of butchering the buffalo for our tribal powwow."

"Really. What kind of knives do you use?" I said.

"Different knives. We often use fillet knives. It's a ceremony."

"I suppose it's just for the tribe," I said.

"No, it's open to the public. You should come."

"We're the kind of people who just might," I replied. "Where did you say you were from again?"

Our second day involved less highway grinding and more pleasant touring. I'm tempted to call it our wildlife day. After making a few stops at pullouts along the upper rim of the Badlands, we took a gravel road twelve miles to Sage Creek Campground. Along the way we saw a big horned sheep, hundreds of prairie dogs, and a ferruginous hawk—a species

I'd never seen before. It was probably looking for a careless prairie dog to eat for lunch. At the spur leading to the campground the other car spotted three red-headed woodpeckers in a small grove of cottonwoods, while just ahead, we were coming upon our first magpie, which had hopped into the shade under a van as we approached.

It was hot in the noon-time glare of the treeless campground, and I was glad we hadn't spent the night there. A few tents were scattered over the dusty expanse, but one of the women hanging out in the shade of a ramada said, "Last night this place was packed!"

On our way out we were stopped by a herd of buffalo desultorily crossing the road. I should have been admiring them but I was impatient to get going, and I started to wonder if the two cars bollixed up ahead of us were enthralled by the beasts or simply too timid to make their way through.

Studying the map a few minutes earlier, we had decided to have lunch in Farmingdale. When we arrived we discovered there was nothing in Farmingdale. We next chose Hermosa as a rendezvous, but the most appealing place we could find there was a deli in a casino-cum-truck-stop called the Flying J.

It was 2 p.m. and we were glad to get in out of the sun for a while. I got a ham and cheese sandwich in a cellophane wrapper and a plastic container of baked beans. They both would have been better if I'd micro-waved them—the bun was on the verge of being frozen—but with loads of mustard and mayo and a big bag of barbecue potato chips, the "meal" was satisfactory.

Tim and Carol, more adventurous, purchased a chicken-fried steak sandwich, with the thought that if it was good, they'd buy a second one. They each took a single bite and then, by mutual consent, tossed it in the garbage. Hilary, going further out on a limb, bought a sausage wrapped in pastry dough with jalapeños and cheese that was sitting under a heat lamp—a glorified pig-in-a-blanket, one of the specialties of the deli.

I think the do-it-yourself root beer floats oozing out of a big do-it-yourself machine may have been the big hit of the occasion. "We're going to get one of those machines for the house," Tim said.

Just south of Hermosa we turned west on Highway 36 and were almost instantly engulfed in a wonderland of rising hills, green pastures, and shadowed pine woods. The sudden contrast was extraordinary, and welcome. We forked over the entry fee at the park gate—$20 per car—and made our way along the narrow winding road through the open woods to the Needles and on to Sylvan Lake.

At one point we spotted some mountain goats on the rocks just above the road. And at the Sylvan Lake Lodge we ordered drinks and sat on the terrace in the late afternoon shade discussing whether there might be a limit to how many birds could bear a single individual's name. For example, after the Swainson's hawk and Swainson's thrush, does the ornithological union cut Swainson off? But what about the Wilson's phalarope, the Wilson's snipe, and Wilson's warbler!

The subject came up because I'd mentioned that I was surprised there weren't any Clark's nutcrackers anywhere nearby—it seemed like perfect habitat—and went on to say that the bird was named after William Clark of "Lewis and Clark" fame.

The lodge is small but nice—a large fieldstone lobby with timbered furniture, a quaint bar, and a well-lit dining room beyond—but the terrace doesn't have much of a view. And they were piping pop music out past the ponderosa pines! I think the Sons of the Pioneers or Commander Cody and His Lost Planet Airmen would have been more appropriate.

On our way back to the car I spotted three big whitish birds attacking the cones in a tree alongside the parking lot.

"What are they?" Carol shouted. (They were parked on the other side of the lot.)

"Clark's nutcrackers," I replied.

"Next time, you should bring up the subject of ivory-billed woodpeckers," she said.

It was a ten-minute ride south to Custer, an attractive tourist town where Gayle had booked a suite of rooms at the Rocket Motel six months earlier. It was actually a single long room with the bathroom placed in the middle, which made the two sleeping areas more private. The rooms were small but immaculate, and the tile work in the bathroom was superb.

The receptionist had only a single key to give the five of us, which proved to be a problem later. But the motel's great strength was its covered terrace, where, as the sun went down, we could sit at patio tables and watch the world go by on Main Street just below us.

A winsome couple and their two kids sat down at the next table to eat a pizza they'd picked up in town.

"This isn't the pizza we ordered," the man said as he opened the box, though he didn't seem very upset. "There's no pineapple on it."

"That means someone else got *our* pizza," his son said astutely. "Well, I guess we might as well eat it."

"So, you're here to see the eclipse?" the man called over to us. "Where ya from?"

We told him. He and his wife had flown to Denver from San Diego with their two kids. "Did you hear they banned double-semis from the freeways in Colorado and put construction projects on hold to alleviate congestion? They say a million people are headed this way. We decided it would be easier to drive north of the totality line and ease back into it from this direction."

They had been hearing stories as they passed through the small towns on the path of totality. "In Agate," the woman said, "they've been discussing such things as how to respond to someone who wants to sacrifice a chicken during the eclipse. Is that legal? These towns aren't used to all the attention. They've been preparing for years."

The eclipse had been calculated to commence at 10:30 the next morning (mountain time) and we were two and a half hours away according to Google Maps. I had been thinking that under normal conditions we'd have plenty of time if we got up at 6, but after a bit of discussion we decided to set our alarm clocks for 3:30 and try to leave Custer by 4. Carol located an all-night convenience store in town on her phone—the Corner Pantry—where we could get some coffee in the morning, and before going to bed we spent a few minutes relaxing in the hot tub adjoining the terrace, confident that all the pieces were falling into place nicely.

It was at this point that we inadvertently locked ourselves out of the room.

THE BIG DAY

I LOVE THE MUFFLED sounds of early morning, when your mind is like cotton and your body is stumbling around on "safe" mode, not yet fully booted. Get up, get dressed, get packed, and get out: that's all you have to do. Stepping outside into the cool night air, I noticed that on the street below, someone had driven a big white pickup truck up onto the curb. (I think he may have been delivering papers to the corner newspaper dispenser.) We were soon headed downtown on Mt. Rushmore Blvd. to the Corner Pantry, which turned out to be a well-lit Conoco gas station stocked with plenty of sugary donuts and rubbery breakfast burritos. The coffee pots seemed to be empty, however.

"I'm making some more right now. It will be ready in a second," the manager said. She was thin as a rail, heavily tattooed, and looked to be about sixteen. Several of us noticed that the cream dispenser squirted cream sideways, and when I mentioned it to her, she said, "I clean that every hour. It just sticks out of the bag funny." She was definitely on the ball.

We headed out of town going south at 4:15. The main drag soon turned into Highway 385, otherwise known as the Gold Rush Byway, which would take us all the way to Alliance. It was pitch black, and there were very few cars on the road. The landscape was shrouded in fog. The tail lights of our companion car soon disappeared around the bends ahead of us, only to reappear on the straightaways, growing ever smaller.

Rounding one bend, we came upon an elk standing in the road, but he moved aside into the ditch a split second before I tapped the horn.

The town of Hot Springs seemed to go on forever in the dark, and it struck me that many of the limestone buildings whizzing by in front of the headlights as we wove our way through it might have been worth seeing in daylight.

Semis passed us occasionally, but as light came gradually to the sky and the fog lifted, the tone remained hushed. Gayle, who was in the other car, texted Hilary as we approached Chadron, and we pulled into the Conoco station on the outskirts of town where they were already parked.

We were now an hour north of Alliance. Traffic continued to be light, almost nonexistent. As the sun rose it transformed the fog itself into a thin diaphanous blanket. At one point four large dark birds flew across the highway ahead of the car. My first thought was cormorants, but then I got a better look at the bills. "Hey, look," I said, "Ibises!"

That was the only unusual thing we saw until we passed a makeshift sign pointing the way to Carhenge. At the next intersection three men were ushering cars into a field. The fee: $10. It was easy to see that the "guests" were being lined up like sardines in anticipation of a big turnout, but the field was less than a quarter full. It was not an appealing scene.

We turned left on the gravel road past the makeshift gate and continued east, passing several similar pay-and-park operations, and turned south on the next section road. We were looking for Madison Road, which sounded important but was no different from the other gravel roads in the vicinity. A mile or so east and we arrived at Sugar Farm.

It might have been 9 a.m. Two young boys emerged from a very small tent as we pulled up. Just beyond them I could see tents and trailers in the pastures, amply spaced and uniformly enveloped in a thin cloud of radiant mist. Bright blue portapotties punctuated the landscape. One of the boys called his mother, and we met up with her at a shed we'd passed on the way in. Tim and I forked over our twenty dollar bills and she scratched our names off a hand-written list.

"They call our place 'sugar ranch' because we fatten up our livestock real well," she told us, "but some people call it 'disabled acres.' That's because we like to buy disabled cows, fatten them up real good, and then eat them ourselves."

Looking out across the field behind us, I asked her about the condition of the terrain.

"Oh, I drive my Nissan all over the place out there. It's all pretty firm, though there are a few bumpy patches. The ground's a little higher over there by the fence."

Indeed, the area by the fence looked good, and we headed over, skirting a shallow pond along the way. One trailer stood fifty yards to the north, and a gravel road cut through the property twenty-five yards to the south. To the east we could see the distant roof of a ranch building half a mile away.

There was still dew on the grass, and it sparkled in the hazy morning light. We parked our cars next to one another, but far enough apart to give us plenty of room between them to sit. For the next two hours, this enclave became our little home, office, laboratory, and lounge.

And it was perfect. Carol got out her knitting; Gayle and Hilary made a pin-hole camera out of a paper plate. Tim pulled out an umbrella, to protect his sensitive Irish skin from the glare. I read a few pages out loud about Lawrence Welk's early years in North Dakota from Ian Frazier's *Great Plains*.

I was totally entranced by the scene; I had never seen vehicles, mobile homes, tents, and people spread out more randomly across the countryside, or with greater intelligence and taste. But our only near neighbor didn't share that opinion. The first time I looked over his way, he made a gesture with upturned hands as if to say, "What? Are you going to park there?" As if we were blocking his view of the sky. His dog had started barking the moment we arrived.

"Yes, we are," I nodded, adding those facial gestures that mean, "Why not?"

The dog eventually quieted down. Hilary and Gayle went over to chat a few minutes later and learned that the man had been parked in that spot for three days. I guess by now he was feeling a little proprietary. I was happy when I saw his wife and daughter emerge from the trailer. It suddenly seemed less likely that he'd unleash the dog on us or pull a shotgun out of the cab.

For the next hour we chatted, goofed around, took some posed photos that I later photoshopped into a group picture, wandered over to the porta-potty, and watched bands of clouds appear, pass overhead, and continue on to the southeast. Both Gayle and Carol consulted their phones repeatedly for the latest weather report.

Right on schedule—surprise, surprise—the disc of the moon took a very slim bite out of the sun. Distant voices cheered and whooped. A half hour later the fields started to look pale, then a little shadowy, then fairly dark. Clouds passed across the face of the sun from time to time and drifted on.

It took about an hour to complete the celestial meal. One moment the moon had largely covered the sun, and the next it had popped completely over it, creating a fiery golden doughnut overhead.

What can you say? It was cool. People cheered in the distance. We opened a bottle of wine. The sky above our heads was a rich, deep blue, while the horizon was lit as if by a purple sunset in every directions. Hilary noticed that most of the cattle on the far side of the road were lying down.

But such moments are impossible to seize. Photos of fiery rings or leaping coronas don't come close. The effect is largely environmental rather than astronomical. It's simultaneously rare and insignificant. There is no way to wrap your head around it, and due to that fact, such events are often infused not only with awe and a giddy kind of joy but also with instant nostalgia. Soon this will all be over.

Then it *is* over. Here comes the sun again. We just saw this movie, except in reverse. Twenty minutes after that brief two-minute span of totality, the light was merely pale and strange again, and all the cows were back on their feet. Ten minutes later, with the eclipse still unwinding itself, our irritable neighbor had already packed up his chairs and his family and driven off.

We lingered in the after-shadow, looking up occasionally with the specially designed glasses from NASA, decorated with an American flag, that Gayle had distributed to us all back in March. It had been an event to remember.

Two hours later, as we drove into Chadron State Park, we spotted Max and Leslie, a couple we often see at concerts in Minneapolis. Turns out they're eclipse chasers. This was their eleventh. They had gathered that evening with friends from the Netherlands and Australia whom they'd met at previous eclipse events.

I don't think I'll ever become an eclipse-chaser myself. It was a marvelous excuse for an excursion, but if I had to chose between the eclipse itself or the four-day road trip with old friends, I'd forego the two minutes of midday darkness, awesome though it was, and keep the trip.

Twenty-eight Ticks

Scientists love numbers. They often have what can only be called a sentimental preference for precision and cleanliness.

I like numbers, too. It's an easy means of comparing things or gauging the relative success of an enterprise. For example, last year we saw 115 bird species on our spring birding trip, while this year we saw 128.

Does that mean that one trip is better than the other? Not really. But it's a useful shorthand. Meanwhile, only a few sightings stand out from any such venture: the scarlet tanager in the trees at the top of the bluff south of Winona; the immature red-tailed hawk fiercely consuming a songbird before our eyes in Trempealeau; the flock of sharp-tailed grouse we inadvertently flushed at Namekagon Barrens.

Hilary and I were hiking on the Superior Hiking Trail in Gooseberry Falls State Park the other day, a mile upstream from the Fifth Falls. We came across an elegant Canada warbler up there, which is a rare treat. (It put my annual warbler count at nineteen—a good year for me.) I also saw a merlin.

The trail follows the river, and from time to time we would stop, sit down on a rocky shelf at the riverbank, take off our boots, cool our feet in the water rushing by, and look for ticks.

On our way back down the hill, we took a two-mile detour

across an upland circle loop. I saw my first black-throated blue warbler along that trail many years ago. I have only seen two or three since.

Our best sighting on this visit was a flock of grouse. The babies flew up from the tall grass one after another and hurried across the broad trail to position themselves in the shadowy branches of the pines growing on the other side of the path. They looked to me like supermarket capons, not only due to their small size but also because they didn't have many feathers.

The father started making a commotion in the woods nearby, fanning his tail and ruffing out the black collar that gives him his name: ruffed grouse. It was an explosive event, and it lasted quite a while, because the babies didn't flush all at once, but individually and unexpectedly, like a sputtering, misdirected roman candle. I think there may have been eight chicks in all.

That trail eventually took us back to the river, and we were eager to sit on the bank again and inventory the impressive harvest of ticks we'd collected as we plodded through the tall grass. By the time I was through examining my socks, legs, and pants, my count had risen to twenty-one.

We mentioned to the ranger at the visitor's center that we'd flushed a family of grouse. She smiled and nodded but I could tell she wasn't impressed, or even much interested. She probably hears such stories every day.

Returning to camp, we ate some smoked fish sandwiches we'd bought in Duluth and then took an evening walk across the huge rocky slab that extends out into Lake Superior— one of my favorite places. The frogs were chorusing from the pools that collect on the rocks, and the stiff grass that fringes the pools caught the low rays of evening light, creating a sublime effect. Two loons were drifting aimlessly out on the lake.

Far more strange was the yellow-headed blackbird I spotted poking around in the pools on the rock shelf. I associate this bird with the cattails and marshes of southern Minnesota, though I seldom see one even there. But with nature, you never know. Perhaps this bird had developed a taste for frogs?

Back at our campsite, I made a fire and we listened to fifteen minutes of rock-and-roll hits from the 70s that were booming from a site at least 200 yards away. Then quiet returned, or at any rate the pleasant sounds of children shrieking, laughing, and shouting as they chased their siblings and cousins around, blithely unaware that the mysteries of twilight were entering deep into their souls. I came across two more ticks during that time; they were plodding up my leg. Ticks often appear out of nowhere, but they're never in a hurry.

We hit the hay before the first stars came out. Slept well. No owls, whippoorwills, or coyotes.

I got up once to answer the call of nature. I wouldn't have mentioned it, except that it serves to explain how, when I got out of my sleeping bag the next morning, I had five more ticks on my legs.

Grand total—twenty-eight.

Let's hope it wasn't twenty-nine.

BWCA Idyll

"The potential for salvation lies where there is danger."

At least, so says the Geman romantic poet Hölderin. When I head to the BWCA, however, I'm not looking for salvation or danger. Yet perhaps Hölderin's remark explains why Seagull Lake is among my favorites. It offers danger of the most serene and attractive kind.

Its broad expanse of open water, three or four miles across, is rendered even more beautiful on a calm sunny morning in July by the numerous islands sitting at odd distances both along the shore and out in the middle. An island you take to be large and distant turns out to be rather small and close by, and vice versa. It's impossible to tell when you're halfway across the lake, but when you're out in the middle there is an enormous amount of water around and underneath you, powerful and threatening if you can wrap your head around it, like a clutch of distant galaxies on a clear dark night, yet also clear and clean and shimmering silvery blue. Seagull Lake offers an enormous space into which the heart can expand, and it comes with a soundtrack: ten or fifteen gulls squawking and screeching as they twirl in the cool morning air around the lump of bare rock well out in the lake where they nest.

Paddling across such immensity for an hour or two,

watching the configuration of islands shift and the far end of the lake take on body by infinitesimal degrees, gives you a truly joyous feeling.

When the wind comes up, not so much. Therein lies the danger. On a windy day the lake can be impossible to traverse. This is especially troublesome when you're at the southwest end and need to get back to the landing.

One of the many great things about the computer age is that you can sit at home, call up the hour-by-hour weather forecast for Seagull Lake, and see how strong the wind will be blowing, and in what direction, ten days from now. I wouldn't put too much stock in such a forecast, but it gives you slightly more confidence, having booked an entry permit, that you'll have a good time once you get there.

On our recent visit, we did. The weather was mild the entire trip, with a thunderstorm each afternoon to add some spice and cool the air.

On our first morning we hit the water at 8 a.m., having camped at Trail's End the night before, and we negotiated the labyrinth of islands at the north end of the lake without difficulty.

After passing those massive cliffs they call the Palisades, we decided to cut behind Miles Island, which would make it easier to move down the west side of the lake. In the back of my mind, I was also thinking about a campsite on a rock shelf down around that corner. I'd passed it many times; it always looked fabulous from a distance but I'd never seen it close up because it had always been occupied.

This time it was vacant. It *was* fabulous. We took it. (What? You've only been on the water for half an hour!)

Once we'd set up camp, we headed back out down the

lake for a mile or two, just to be out on that glorious expanse in the freshness of the morning: recreational paddling. We examined a few vacant campsites for future reference and arrived back at camp at 10:30. Perfect.

Camp life is often simple. When you think of something to do, you usually go off and do it, without a great deal of logistical analysis. For example: "I think I'll go out and get some water." So you paddle well out into the bay, beyond the beaver thoroughfares, throw the plastic bucket over the side of the canoe, and haul up some water. Or: "I think I'll go get some firewood." And off you go into the woods with your collapsible aluminum saw. But you haven't actually assembled the saw. There's precious little firewood to be found in the BWCA these days. You probably won't need it.

In any case, it doesn't matter. You do your cooking on a stove, and staring into a campfire tends to be less interesting during the long days of midsummer than watching night descend.

Such chores having been completed, you're free to immerse yourself in the changing patterns of color on the surface of the water, or go in for a swim, or pick a few blue-berries—one of Hilary's specialties.

Sitting on coarse rock,
I splash my body with water.
They've known each other forever.

The clouds are a source of continual fascination. A pair of eagles is hanging around a large nest in a dead tree on the island just across the channel. Usually they're doing nothing, just like you. But they might do something soon. Just like you.

But camp life isn't quite so simple as it seems. As the sun moves across the sky, parts of the campsite that were in shade become bathed in sunlight. If you happen to be sitting in such a spot, you're going to have to move. Thus the day becomes a pageant of shifting locales and perspectives.

Bright sun trying
to penetrate the white pine boughs
gentle breeze lends a hand

Two rangers stopped by to check our permit.

"Hey, we passed you two going the other way early this morning amid the islands," I said.

"Yup. That was us." Discerning that we're experienced campers (or just old) one of them inquired if we'd been on the lake before.

"The first time I was on Seagull was 1964," I said.

"I was born in 1989, so you got me on that one," he replied with a smile. He had a long sandy beard that didn't look quite so Millennial out here in the brush.

"We like to ask people with experience how things have changed over the years," he said.

"Not much, really," I said. "It's as beautiful as ever. Maybe a little more crowded. Hence the need to make camp early." I might have mentioned that fifty years ago there was a big wooden forest service sign at every portage with letters carved into it, painted yellow: Gillis Lake, 44 rods. And there seem to be fewer Canada jays lurking around the campsites than there used to be. And fewer moose, of course.

"About the same? That's good to hear," he said. "Er, do you mind if I go out and measure the depth of the latrine?"

"By all means. Be my guest."

* * *

After a simple lunch of freeze-dried peanuts, some obscure hard Spanish goat cheese on coarse Wasabröt crackers, and Kool-Aid, we settle in to do some reading. In Ernst Cassirer's *An Essay on Man* I almost immediately hit upon a passage about memory that seemed relevant to the day.

> *In man we cannot describe recollection as a simple return of an event, as a faint image or copy of a former impression. It is not simply a repetition but a rebirth of the past; it implies a creative and a constructive process. It is not enough to pick up isolated data of our past experiences, we must really recollect them, we must organize and synthesize them, and assemble them into a focus of thought.*

But this is a bit backward, don't you think? We don't assemble memories into a focus of thought willfully, or at random. Rather, we begin with a problem or issue or focus of thought, and then comb our memories in an effort to illuminate or come to terms with it. That may explain why our humiliations, which we remain concerned about and wish we could erase, tend to be more vivid in memory than our triumphs.

Often the constructive process Cassirer refers to results in a narrative—a story leading to a moral or an exclamation of wonderment or horror. If only we had time to tell that story! If only we could make it sound good. If only anyone would listen! These stories enter our "recall holding tank" as tape loops that we can retrieve as soon as some interlocutor's reference "reminds us" of them. Then off we go with a sequential replay.

The ranger mentioned that campsites had filled up early the previous night on Ogishkemuncie Lake, discomfitting four or five parties that had arrived at 5 p.m. hoping to camp there. The remark recalled to my mind that once-beautiful lake. When I was just a kid our Scout troop camped there for a week. One day a few of us "discovered" Mueller Falls. I remember a shake-jar half-full of blueberries and the ominous, distant roar of we knew not what. Earlier in the afternoon, we had waded up the river, dragging our canoe brutally over a short wide waterfall, and paddled around in the pool above it. Intrigued by the growing rumble, we continued upstream. We rounded a corner and there it was: an impressive and hitherto unknown waterfall. I was old enough at the time to be reading Edgar Rice Borroughs, and this experience fit right in.

When we got back to camp, we told the adults excitedly about our discovery. "Oh, you found Mueller Falls," one of them said with a chuckle. They were amused, but hardly astounded. As a result, *they* became less godlike in my eyes.

Cassirer remarks that impressions have to be "ordered and located" and "referred to different points in time." That isn't exactly true, either. The older we get, the less solid the chronology of our memories becomes. Whether something happened three years ago or eight years ago is hard to recall. The memories have become narratives, then myths. Pleasant myths, if all has gone well.

Hilary and I have camped on Seagull Lake at least eight times, maybe more. How do I know? By counting up the campsites we've occupied. The little red dots on the map help, though one small island we camped on is no longer marked as a site. Several of the sites are associated in my mind with an event—the supernova site, the high wind site, the small island site, the Canada jay site, the spruce grouse site, and the loon line site, among others. *When* did we camp at these places, scattered here and there across the lake? I couldn't tell you. Does it matter?

Shared memories have a value beyond the ordinary. We bring them up to revive personal connections, though the person we're sharing them with might be thinking, "That's not what happened." Criminal investigators are well aware that eye-witness accounts are among the least reliable forms of evidence. And people invariably remember different details about the same event, after all, and read different things into them.

* * *

Monday morning. Not a cloud in the sky. We were on the water at eight once again, having said goodbye to the pesky chipmunks, the local robin, and the chipping sparrow who's raising a family on the far side of the bushes near shore. The eagles were nowhere to be seen.

There was a gentle breeze out on the lake, where we soon met up with our eagle family, engaged in an airborne feud with a dozen gulls near the bare rock island that the gulls, if they could talk, would probably call home. The gulls, screeching and keening, were attacking the eagles high above the surface of the water. The eagles would make an occasional turnabout, but no one seemed to be making contact. The battle lasted for fifteen minutes and was still going on as we paddled beyond earshot. It's probably been going on for eons.

We were hoping to get the crescent-shaped campsite at the south east corner of the open lake, where we've camped at least three times in previous years. As we approached, we both pulled our binoculars out and combed the site for the flash of bright color that would indicate a tent, a tarp, or a life preserver hung thoughtfully in a tree. Closer and closer, but everything looked green and gray and natural.

I'm sitting at that campsite right now. Hilary has gone in for a swim, we've broken into a bag of gorp, and now she's headed off up the hill looking for blueberries.

We arrived here at 10:30—a more respectable time to quit paddling, but only slightly.

* * *

It's seldom commented on in rhapsodic books about the BWCA how much time visitors spend in a mental stupor. Or maybe it's just me. In larger groups people always seem to be shouting back and forth between canoes. They're out paddling while Hilary and I are sitting on the rocks in our camp chairs, constructed by slipping our Thermo-rest pads into small light-weight webbed frames designed for that purpose. I look out across the lake or follow every move of some bird or rodent in an effort to figure out what he or she is up to. I read a few lines from a book, stare at a passing ant, or admire the lichen covering the rock under my left knee.

Yesterday the afternoon was enlivened by a few thunderheads. They drifted southeast before the rain commenced, though we got enough of the downpour to send us scurrying into the tent briefly. Thunderbolts were isolated and abrupt, full-bodied, sonorous, Zeus-like. I saw only a single bolt of lightning: thin, a long way off in the gray sheet of sky to the south where it was raining hard. Once the storm moved past we returned to our rock shelf where, above our heads, swirling strands of hair-like clouds, a pure bluish white, were trailing off the back of the passing thunderhead into the clear blue sky behind it. A few minutes later a feeble half-rainbow appeared to the east.

The chipmunks, usually tireless and tenacious, had vanished, spooked by the thunder, perhaps.

* * *

While we're on the subject of yesterday—I neglected to mention the beautiful magnolia warbler we saw, or the red-breasted nuthatch, more of a sleek slate gray than I'm used to seeing. And the flat-headed robin who nabbed little dragonflies in his beak repeatedly, hopped around on the rocks for a few seconds, then flew off across the channel to the island where his offspring were no doubt creating a racket in their nest.

* * *

I have noticed that sometimes the waterbugs cluster together, as if they're exchanging information, experiences, memories. At other times they skim across the water seemingly at random, widely dispersed.

* * *

Once again a mild clear morning produces a mid-afternoon thunderstorm. Once again I notice that as the clouds pass overhead, the wind rises and reverses direction, though the clouds above continue on their original course. Today the rain was more severe and the fetch across the lake was much greater. Soon whitecaps were coming in our direction from the east. As we lay in the tent, I said, almost idly, "I wonder if I should go out and tie up the canoe?"

That's always a good idea, though our canoe was drawn up on shore in a natural harbor on the leeward side of the peninsula, shallow and virtually surrounded by swamp laurel bushes. All the same, I put on my sandals and raincoat and headed out into the wind and rain. When I sighted the canoe it was ten feet from shore, bobbing out to sea at a surprising clip. I was dumbstruck. I splashed out into the water and grabbed it, dragged it into the harbor again, and flipped it over with an emphatic thud, as if to say, "And don't you try anything like that again!"

* * *

Sky clears. Back to my camp chair, avoiding the puddles, I turn once again to Cassirer, and read:

> *He who lives in harmony with his own self, his daemon, lives in harmony with the universe; for both the universal order and the personal order are nothing but different expressions and manifestations of a common underlying principle. Man proves his inherent power of criticism, of judgment, and discernment, by conceiving that in this correlation the Self, not the Universe, has the leading part.*

Cassirer is talking here about a concept that runs from Socrates to Marcus Aurelius, namely, human judgment regarding beauty, truth, and goodness. A reader might easily move on from these remarks to whatever comes next, oblivious to its import, but when you copy out a paragraph longhand, phrase by phrase, it's hard to avoid pausing to consider whether what's being said is true. The word that catches my eye here is "principle." The reality and importance of harmony between inner and outer I can accept, because I've felt it. Whether that harmony rests on a mere principle I very much doubt. Rather, that harmony must rely on a *force*. Philosophers have been struggling for millennia to come up with a principle to describe that force, but the two are not the same thing, any more than the force of gravity is the same thing as the formula that describes it.

What is the force binding inner and outer life? It's the

love force, of course. Thus philosophy is reduced to a Beatles song. Well, why not?

I'm feeling the force right now. The air has grown much clearer since the storm. A gorgeous clarity. Hilary is sitting here beside me with her watercolors, and three gulls are circling overhead, shrieking pleasantly. Each passing moment is a nugget of delight about which I can do nothing except jot a few feeble notes in a journal. Or draw a picture.

A second issue presents itself, however. Does the Self really play the leading part in what Cassirer describes as a "correlation" between it and the Universe? Or do the two inform one another mutually, or even dialectically? Perhaps all Cassirer is trying to say is that the Self is not a product or derivative or miniature of the universe, but a being that can envision forms of beauty and truth that have never before been given substance, and not only envision them, but bring them to life. Hence the significance of incarnation, in all its forms.

* * *

Dawn is great, though after three nights in a tent, maybe the Self is not so great. The Universe is getting the upper hand, I'm afraid. Still, the elements exude that harmony we never cease to love. A glow in the east across two miles of open water. It's the dawn of creation...with granola and prunes and a second cup of coffee, very strong. It takes fifteen minutes to make the coffee through a hand-held Melitta filter, but we've got time. The wind is gentle, and it's at our back.

We'll cross the lake alright.

The Boule Party

It's become a tradition as ingrained in the summer season as a trip to the state fair: the annual boule party hosted by our friends Carol and Tim. It's an afternoon backyard event that invariably extends well into the evening centered around food, conversation, and the game of *pétanque*. I consider myself lucky to be a part of a circle of friends many of whom I've known since college days—that's going back a ways. We all converge in the Wahl's backyard on the Saturday of Labor Day weekend, joined by various of the player's children, and in recent years grandchildren. The center of attention is the boule court that Tim has constructed in the backyard, lined with slabs of Kasota limestone and filled with fine gravel of a uniform consistency. I'm sure it's heavy work, digging the bed, laying the border, and hauling the gravel, though Tim has chosen to do most of it himself. Many of us have offered to help, over the years, and a few of us have, but I understand Tim's rationale for mostly working alone: you've got to do some work, then step back, ponder the next step, unhurried and unburdened by the responsibility of keeping other workers occupied.

I might add that since they initiated the annual event, Tim and Carol have moved twice. After their most recent move, another long-time participant and three-time champion, Jim Ingebretsen, suggested to me that we create an award to honor the Herculean labor of building a backyard court for yet a third time. The result was a beautiful certificate with an image of Tim christening the previous court with a glass of red wine, over which I superimposed the following text.

Après avoir terminé la construction
du troisième terrain de
pétanque, conforme aux exigences de
la Societé Internationale de Constructeurs et Ingenieurs de terrains
de pétanque, nous vous conférons le très prestigieux titre maître
constructeur de terrains de pétanque ainsi que tous les privilieges et
droits qui accompagnent une telle honneur.

I believe this is genuine French. I sent the English text I'd written to our friend Rollo, who's fluent in the language, and he sent me this corrected version. (Rollo now lives in Seattle, alas, and makes the late summer gathering only occasionally.) There are so many cognates in there—"after having completed the construction of the third boules court...confer the prestigious title...all the rights and privileges...etc., etc.", that it hardly seems necessary to translate it.

The new court is longer than the first two were, and after the first competition on it, Tim, feeling that it had too much of a slant, took the entire thing apart and hired someone with a Bobcat to come in and level the soil. This is serious business, in a playful way, and it reminds me of a remark attributed to the Spanish philosopher José Ortega y Gasset: "The superfluous is in every way more necessary than the necessary."

The game itself is so simple that children can play—and they often do. The idea is to get your ball closer to the target ball—the *cochonnet*—which is thrown out by one of the competitors at the start of each point, than your opponent does.

Once there are two or three balls lying on the court in front of the *cochonnet*, it becomes difficult to ease another one past; it's sometimes a better idea to simply knock your opponent's ball further down the court. Easier said than done.

Some participants prefer to loft the small metal ball quite a ways down the court, often giving it a bit of backspin to ensure that it doesn't roll too far once it lands. Other players depend entirely on rolling the ball, hoping to maintain the right "line" and distance across the slightly bumpy court. To some degree, which delivery you use depends on the situation at hand. And fatigue. And the wine.

The balls are about the size of a baseball, but made of shiny steel, I think. Three of them have a few lines scored into the surface; the other three have lots of lines circling them in both directions. Thus the game takes on a few overtones of pre-socratic philosophy: the few and the many.

Or maybe that's just the way I look at it. Underlying this grand annual event more broadly is an appreciation for European peasant life shared by most, if not all, of the contestants. Sitting at a café table upon which sits a glass of Pernod and maybe a basket of bread, with a lively boule game taking place nearby, is an ideal drawn from the novels of Ford Madox Ford and John Berger, the films of Jean Renoir, and the mysteries of Martin Walker, among many other sources. But unlike Civil War reenacters (for example) who dress up in antique uniforms and pretend to fight bloody battles, the boule party isn't "pretend." It has been, from the beginning, an organic part of everyday living among a group of widely travelled friends. You're more likely to see a Hawaiian shirt there than a Basque beret. And although the game we're playing is French, a variety of European flavors and influences has always been present, typified by Rocky's Serbian *cevapcici*. She's been bringing these sausages of ground pork, beef, and lamb, made from a cherished family recipe, right from the first, I think, with husband Greg tending the grill, and they're always a hit.

Although the boules competition ostensibly lies at the heart of the afternoon festivities, you could be standing around for hours before tossing your first ball, especially if you happened to get a first-round bye. And if you lose that first round, you're done for the day. A few of us spend some time officiating, measuring distances between the balls and the *cochonnet* to determine who's won a point, and raking the court after each series of tosses. It can also be fun to sit alongside the court and dispense commentary and wise and witty advice to those who are still in the running. Equally important is the food, the drink, and especially the idle backyard conversations that take place here and there throughout the day.

One subject that resurfaces again and again in the course of a typical afternoon's conversation is travel. Mostly upcoming travel. At our most recent gathering, Tim and Carol were leaving the next morning for a three-week tour of Croatia, Jeff and Fran were on their way to Ireland, Hilary and I were heading for Nova Scotia, Becca and David were going on an educational cruise around Greece, Michel and Renie were attending an academic conference in Vancouver (though not until February), and Jim and Debbie were off on a camping excursion to Manitoba with their Vistabule trailer.

It's hard to reconstruct such events in detail, but I can recall chatting with Lisa about a concert she and her husband, Dave, gave at the Como Park Pavilion with the White

Bear Big Band a few weeks earlier; the elderly tenor saxophonist next to her knew his part and played it well, but he
has memory problems and Lisa had to prompt him again and
again as to what to do next. I spoke at length with Emma and
Jessie about their backyard garden and their recent trip to the
BWCAW—his first. They had trouble finding a campsite on
Rose Lake and Jesse's overall reaction to the experience was
a cheerful "What's the point?" I chatted with Rocky about
the staunch commitment that high school teachers often
feel toward their careers and their students. I mentioned to
Jim, who's interested in Scandinavian literature, a book by a
Swede I'd read recently called *The Fly Trap*. He countered
with a book about bumblebees he'd just been reading called
A Sting in the Tail. I asked Brianna about her job as a public
defender, her determination to pay off her enormous student
loans, and her efforts to help her husband, who's Mexican,
gain entry to the United States. I asked Turner, a film buff,
if he'd seen *Once Upon a Time in Hollywood* yet. "It's on my
list," he said drolly. His sister, Abigail, came over and we got
to talking about Quentin Tarantino, a director I don't much
like. They both recommended *Jackie Brown*. Gayle told me
a bit about her recent trip to her daughter's upscale lodge in
the Cascade Mountains; it often floods, unfortunately, and
she and her husband are in the process of suing the previous
owners. Michel and I, as usual, started out with a grandiose
metaphysical canvas before us, but soon enough found ourselves discussing the tremendous shirts we'd picked up recently at second-hand stores. When I mentioned to Fran that
Hilary and I were heading to Nova Scotia soon, she shared
some information about Halifax, where she'd been on business. And Greg gave me a detailed account of a presentation

he made called "A Primer on Carbon-Free Heat Tech" at a user-led technology and software conference that takes place annually at the Best Buy headquarters in Richfield.

Tim was mostly busy dashing here and there, managing the tournament. He instituted a new rule this year. Contestants are now required to toss the ball with both feet inside a circle drawn in the gravel. In previous years only one foot had to be in, which made it easier to move from side to side and find an open pathway to the *cochonnet* around the balls that had already been thrown. I found it constraining at first, but also more challenging, and I ended up liking it a lot.

I've won the tournament two times before, but that was more than a decade ago. My star has long since faded, and the limelight has shifted to others. When I knocked out Greg, the reigning champ, in the first round, it was considered a major upset.

This year Dave, a perennial favorite, also fell from competition in the early rounds, and Jim was knocked out in an intense nip-and-tuck battle with his wife, Debbie. I knocked her out of the competition in the next round, though not without difficulty. Michel outlasted Carol, and Tim continued an exhibition of brilliant sky-balling that Michel could not overcome.

There we were, Tim and I, in the final. Darkness had fallen, and various friends were holding up the flashlights on their phones to illuminate the court. Tim surged to a five-zip lead, but I crawled back into contention. The score eventually stood at seven to eight. I got close. He sent me to the back wall with yet another brilliant sky-ball, then put another one close. With my last ball I had no choice but to try to knock him away. I hit the mark and his metal ball went streaming to the limestone wall. But mine wound up nowhere near the *cochonnet*. Tim rolled a final ball effortlessly within three inches of the little piglet, and the trophy was his.

The final moments of the boule party take place inside, where an extraordinary array of breads, salads, casseroles, and deserts—and also the last of the *civaps*—sit waiting to be distributed. It's the only time when everyone is standing together around the food.

"Who made that shrimp dish? That was great."

"What's in that quinoa salad?"

"Was that yogurt sauce supposed to go with the flatbread?"

Everyone loads a sample or two from various dishes into their own bowl or plate, and off we go into the night, full of love for our friends and gratitude to our hosts, happy to be a part of such a rich and long-standing tradition.

Morning and Evening

These cool summer mornings must be considered great. Or better yet, heavenly.

There's a cardinal on the feeder, I can only see the bottom of his reddish tail, bobbing up and down as he eats.

House wrens chatter in the distance. And the blue jay delivers his submarine chortle from off in the woods.

The goldfinch is fearless, but prudent. He doesn't waste time, just nibbles and leaves, close enough that I can see his dainty orange beak.

Raccoon tracks on the deck. He's been in the ashes of the grill, looking for grease.

Suddenly a plan for the morning takes shape:
– fill the birdbath;
– water the compost pile with the same hose;
– admire the cup flower that's finally blooming after months of clumsy growth.

Then, another cup of coffee.

Down in the yard, I come upon the remains of a robin. Hawks tend to swoop in from the south, nab their prey, and enjoy a meal in privacy on this very spot.

Now it's the sharp "tisk, tisk" of the red squirrel, and a single nuthatch with his nasal "beep-beep." Four chickadees chuckle on the same branch. It's a family! But I don't think they're getting along.

Finally chipmunk arrives. He slept late.

And now all the birds are singing at once! I've never heard anything quite like it, unless it was that morning we were camping in a county park near Northfield. I never found that park again.

You can't really capture the joy of such a morning.

Just keep the windows open, stay away from the computer.

Keep the breeze moving through.

A SUMMER EVENING for grilling steaks and onions on the deck, with sweet potato disks (slathered in olive oil and thyme) roasting in the oven just inside.

It was a cool, clear evening, enhanced by the piercing drone of the cicadas and a minor avalanche of birdlife. All the regulars were out—the chickadees, the goldfinches, a blue jay squawking from the top of a towering spruce, a house finch dressed in an orange shade of red. Chimney swifts chattered in the clear blue sky, then a single common nighthawk appeared, cruising the skies overhead. He is the truest, or at any rate the most dramatic, evening guest, with his emphatic shriek that evokes childhood memories and sends a comforting message: things are alright.

I'm not sure things are alright for the nighthawk, whom we see less often than we used to. They eat flying insects, so it stands to reason that the rise in pesticide use hasn't done them much good. Then again, they often nest on gravel rooftops, which are less popular than they once were. We might reason, therefore, that the nighthawk population gained an artificial boost during the "gravel-roof" period in architectural history, and is now returning to traditional levels.

The nighthawk was recently chosen as Bird of the Year

by the ABA. I'm not sure why. I learned on their website that there are nine subspecies (yikes!) which is a matter of no great concern to those of us who see them in the distance flying overhead at dusk. That's the only way most of us will ever see them.

Its Latin name comes from two Greek roots that in combination mean "musical chord at dusk." Nice. I have never heard anyone use the bird's other common names, such as bullbat, pisk, and will-o'wisp. They sound like archaic terms out of a Charles Frazier novel. Nor have I heard the booming noise the night hawk allegedly makes with its feathers at the end of a steep dive.

The ABA website freely admits that the nighthawk, though often seen, is still poorly understood. Yes, nature is mysterious. I believe the goldfinch is also poorly understood. In particular, we don't really understand how the goldfinch feels about looking like a porcelain bird—stunning but slightly fake. To my eye, goldfinches look more relaxed in the wintertime, when their coloration takes on a muted and more natural shade.

The steaks were good. And a splash or two of wine. Yes. And conversation turns to the subject of death—we had just been to a funeral—and the passage of time, and the precious being of loved ones, which is different from their merit or influence or achievement. Yes. A musical chord at dusk. And on into the night.

September – Washing Windows

Anyone who was outside on Saturday afternoon would agree, it was a perfect day for washing windows.

The biggest challenge Hilary and I face lies with the twelve-pane wooden storm window in the living room, which has been deteriorating little by little for decades. It's a heavy window, and it sits directly above a thick, spreading yew that's difficult to work your way behind. The saving grace is that once we've lifted the window out of its casing and off the sill, we can lower it and set it down on the yew bush. After we've made our way back out from behind the bush into the yard, we can then lift the window again and carry it over to the driveway to be cleaned.

The lower left corner of this massive storm window looked so shaky when we tried to lift it, I was afraid some of the panes were going to fall out. After we'd lugged it across the yard and leaned it against the car, Hilary went inside to get some Gorilla Glue. After a few more trips inside to get a nail, then a pair of pliers, we finally succeeded in reaching some glue that hadn't solidified in the bottle. I applied it to the loose sections of the corner using a toothpick, then squeezed a tablespoon down into the seemingly hollow core of the pane. Then we carefully rotated the window ninety degrees so its weight would bear down forcibly on the newly repaired corner while the glue set.

My job would be to stand by the window, which is roughly five feet tall and seven feet wide, to make sure the wind didn't blow it over. The glue would take quite a while to set, so I had my work cut out for me.

I looked over at the globe cedar that needs sheering, and the zinnias that were laying on the ground, having been beaten down by the recent rains. A blue jay flew overhead, and then I saw some goldfinches across the roof of the house in the oak tree in the back yard.

The leaves of the oak have always been slightly yellow, due, I've been told, to the nutrients lacking in the clay soil hereabouts. I pondered whether it might be a good thing to be rid of that oak tree altogether, but its dead branches offer a variety of perches for the birds as they approach the feeders.

The sky was blue, though there were isolated waves of wispy ice clouds here and there, like white cake decorations applied with a comb.

Hilary had gone inside to wash some other windows, and when she came back out I said, "How long have I been standing here?"

"About ten minutes."

"Is that all?"

"Maybe fifteen."

These are the critical minutes when the glue is setting, and I knew my continued patience would be rewarded. I'm unusually adept at staring off into space for extended periods when there's work to be done. All the same, I was getting bored, and a few minutes later we decided to lift the window again and move it between the two cars. There wasn't much of a breeze anyway, and in that position a rising gust would hit the window harmlessly, face on, rather than waffling down its length.

For the next few minutes we washed pane after pane, using pages torn from old copies of the *New York Review of Books*. In one issue I spotted a three-year-old review by Philip Lopate of a book by Edward Hoagland that I purchased not long ago as a remainder. I set those pages aside.

The glue set remarkably well, as it turns out. After washing the twelve panes on both sides we hoisted the massive window back up onto the yew, then scrambled behind the bush and set it carefully into place again. Magnificent.

A few minutes later, as I was settling in to read that review, I heard a loud thud. A bird had flown into the dining-room window. A thrush now lay motionless on the seat of a metal patio chair, his pale dotted breast exposed. At first I thought it was a veery—an elusive cinnamon-colored bird with an ethereal downward-cascading flute-like song. But I later got to thinking it was a gray-cheeked thrush, due to the drab back and rather prominent spots.

One of the drawbacks of perfectly clean windows is that birds can't see them. Sometimes they hit them. Often they revive; this one didn't. Eventually I carried it down into the yard and set it in the shadows amid the ferns. (We do have translucent hawk decals on the windows. We like to think they help. The theory is that they reflect ultraviolet light, which the birds can see a lot better than we can. They see the images and avoid the glass, while we see little.)

Both veerys and gray-cheeked thrushes spend their winters in Venezuela and north-central Brazil. I wonder if Rima, the bird-spirit in W. H. Hudson's once-famous South American novel, *Green Mansions*, was a veery, though there are plenty of other candidates in the southern hemisphere who never travel this far north.

On a lighter note, when Hilary was wrestling one of the aluminum combination storms back into its track, she noticed a wispy insect climbing the outer pane. It was a grasshopper of some sort, though it was bright green, and looked like it was born yesterday. Its surface looked tender, like a spring leaf, and it was less compact than the standard, yellow-brown grasshoppers that leap off the trail in front of you in late summer.

We watched it climb uncertainly up the glass, taking alternate steps with its four spindly front legs, two by two, while using the two long trailing legs for stability as needed. It continued up to the corner of the window, then proceeded slowly out of sight, up the painted clapboard wall of the house.

Looking it up later, I determined that the creature was a katydid.

"That wasn't a grasshopper, that was a katydid," I shouted to Hilary in the next room.

"It's not CATydid," she shouted back. "It's KAY-tee-did."

Fall

Don't Knock the Equinox!

Plato celebrated the Golden Mean, and gained lasting renown for coining the slogan: Everything in moderation, including moderation.

Saturday was neither the longest nor the shortest day of the year, but the most equanimitous, with daylight and dark bowing and curtsying like dancers in a line.

The equinox isn't something you notice; you merely read about it in the EarthSky News email that appears in your inbox every day, complete with incomprehensible diagrams that remind you of the spatial relations test you took in eighth grade.

What I did notice was that after several days of unrelenting rain, the day dawned cool and bright. It was a spectacular morning, in fact, and Hilary and I decided to head out to the pottery "tour" taking place in the St. Croix Valley.

Our route took us east on I-694, then north on I-35E to the Hugo exit. Hugo has never been much of a town, and the region next to the freeway is now a suburb, but we ought to commend the developers who created that exurban zone for naming one of the prominent streets Victor Hugo Boulevard. The town itself is named after the less eminent Trevanion William Hugo, chief engineer of the Consolidated Elevator Company and mayor of Duluth from 1901 to 1904.

As we drove past a spanking new Quik-Stop gas station

on our way into town, it occurred to me that I ought to read *The Hunchback of Notre Dame* someday.

We continued east on County 4 past marshes, farms, and rolling hills past Big Marine Lake and on to Marine on the St. Croix. The sunlight was still striking, and the air was crystal clear. Some sort of cycling event was taking place—we passed a peloton on the way into town and came upon more cyclists milling around on Judd Street.

At the miniscule public library I asked if they happened to have a de-acquisition shop. No. But they did have a cardboard box of CDs in the lobby that were free for the taking. A few Mozart piano concertos. A historic recording (remastered) of *Aida* with Renata Tebaldi, Teresa Berganza, and Carlo Bergonzi. Why not?

We ascended a staircase next door to the library and discovered an art gallery I'd never seen before operated by one Mary Jo Van Dell, who does very large oil paintings with exquisite lighting and high horizon lines. Alongside the oils she's stocked her gallery with a variety of other artworks—especially hand-thrown local pottery and pine furniture. I was especially taken by the long, untreated pine table and an elegant narrow skiff on the far wall. In fact, the vessel seemed almost too narrow to be seaworthy. An immense *objet 'd 'art*, perhaps? Mary Jo offered us a cup of coffee and invited us into the back room to see her studio.

I might also mention Mary Jo's efforts to open her gallery space to local painters, and her vision to host readings and books club discussions in the open space of the gallery. How many artists, craft specialists, and serious readers ARE there in the vicinity of Marine? I'm guessing quite a few.

A second shop, HWY North, has recently opened up

right across the street, owned and operated (I think) by Emily Anderson. The shop has some stunning art by Tom Maakestad; I especially like the oil pastels. But it also has plenty of locally made jewelry, note cards, candles, kitchen tools, and other such stuff.

Emily had just opened the shop when we arrived. The sun was steaming in the windows. "Let's put on something sunny," she said. "The Beatles!"

"Ah, yes," I replied. "But what about that classic "I'm So Down"?

If Emily caught my gaff, she never let on. I was actually conflating two famous Beatles tunes: "I'm So Tired" and "I'm Down." Rather than embarrass me she graciously replied, "I actually *like* depressing music." Somehow, I doubt it.

I'm especially interested in the Marine Mills Folk School that Emily and some friends are trying to get going at her shop. They've offered classes in pickling, soap-making, boat-building, and other rustic crafts. I would offer to teach one myself, but I can't imagine what the subject would be. "How to Make Acorn Bread"? It isn't worth the effort. "InDesign for Fun and Profit"? Too techie.

Now, Marine is everyone's idea of a cute Minnesota town, and it's also the "gateway" to William O'Brien State Park. But it needed a few galleries and gift shops to bolster its core and give visitors something to DO there. Now it's got those features. Hitherto its most distinctive riverside café was almost impossible to find and its foremost business was the general store, which dates back to the pioneer days of the mid-nineteenth century, before Minnesota was a state. The sandwich specials are always worthwhile, but I have always associated the store with salty snacks. Hilary and I go cross-country skiing at the nearby state park every winter, and after an arduous ski nothing tastes better than a big bag of Ruffles cheddar cheese potato chips.

We spent the next few hours visiting the studios of Jadoonath Pottery, Guillermo Cuellar, and Nick Earl. I love looking at pots, but feel no need to buy one, and in any case, seldom see one that's as interesting as the ones Hilary is making these days. It's also pleasant to soak in the ambiance of potters chatting with one another about kilns, electrical wiring, how many times you ought to rinse Basmati rice before cooking, and other important stuff. Most of those attending the sales seemed to be insiders. Hilary and I are outsiders, though we did have the perspicacity to notice "living master" Warren MacKenzie chatting with friends on a bench at the Cuellar studio.

One of the potters was wearing go-go boots and a quasi-Dakota dress. The only thing missing was a Buffalo Springfield album blaring from a boom-box.

Don't get me wrong. I'm not poking fun at anyone. I'm the kind of guy who loves an open fire, sleeping in a tent on the ground, listening for the whippoorwills, reading Li Po or Machado by starlight. The Revolution has hardly begun. And I get a little upset when I read, in *The New York Review of Books* for example, dismissive comments about how the energy of the radical 60s fizzled.

> *In the longer run, much of the countercultural ferment was absorbed into the therapeutic culture of self-realization or frittered away in the fragmentation bred by identity politics. A counter-cultural sensibility survives behind the ecologically informed awareness that humans must accommodate themselves to the natural world rather than simply master it, but that sensibility remains untethered to any capacious critique of technocratic rationality—one that would include,*

for example, the ever-increasing defense budget or the nuclear arms race. The creators of our public discourse need to recover the counter-cultural critique of the technocratic ethos, which still legitimates the national security state. Without that critique, debate over foreign policy—though conducted in moralistic rhetoric—remains devoid of moral seriousness. Revisiting the religious dimensions of 1960s protest allows for the recovery of a forgotten and necessary part of our past.

Blah, blah, blah. We don't need to recover the past. We need to refashion the future. And people have been doing that for a good long time now. And just you wait and see!

I wonder if the fellow who wrote that passage has ever seen a modern wind turbine. I can tell you one thing: it's not made of untreated pine slabs.

Our final stop was to the Arcola Bluffs Day Use Area, an obscure site on the Arcola Trail—a gravel road that cuts east from the highway toward the river and rejoins it a few miles downstream.

One thing about the St. Croix River is that the countryside thereabouts is pretty, but you never see the river itself. This little park gives you the opportunity to walk down to it through the woods. Which we did.

You finally reach the river just downstream from the Arcola railroad bridge. It's an engineering masterpiece and also a work of art. It was designed by famous bridge engineer C.A.P. Turner, who also designed the Duluth Lift Bridge and the Mendota Bridge. This is America's Eiffel Tower, tucked away amid the water and woods of flyover land.

In my youth I walked out on the Arcola Bridge, high above the river, once or twice.

Kids still go out there, I think. It's not for the faint of heart.

Lanesboro Encore

We see our friends Don and Sherry only a few times a year: once in December for a whirlwind holiday evening of conversation; once in May for a bike trip ostensibly in celebration of our birthdays, all of which happen to fall within a stretch from late March to mid-May; some sort of summer event; and a grand occasion in the fall when we indulge in a two-day biking excursion, usually around World Series time.

It doesn't sound like much, but we've been doing it for 35 years. There is no way, at this late date, to pin down exactly how many years it's been, but it seems to me we've never missed a year, and as I think back on the places we've stayed overnight during those fall weekends, it begins to sound impressive. Our Wisconsin bivouacs have included Trempealeau, Alma, Fountain City, Wilton, Eau Claire, Menomonie, River Falls, Chippewa Falls, New Post, Dresser, Bayfield, and Bailey's Harbor. Our Minnesota adventures have included overnights in Duluth, Little Falls, Nisswa, Sauk Center, Dundas, and Lanesboro.

It might seem that Wisconsin locations are over-represented here, until you factor in all the times we established our base camp in that quaint and appealing Minnesota town of Lanesboro.

Why Lanesboro? Two branches of the Root River flow

through it, it has two theaters, restaurants in every zone from a counter-service pizza place to a one-seating establishment where they serve crostini topped with flying fish roe, a small but top-flight local art gallery, sixty miles of bike trails, Amish farmers selling quilts and pies in the city park with their horses tethered nearby, a genuine livestock market every Friday, a first-rate wild bird store up in the hills just west of town, and a wide variety of affordable accommodations.

If memory serves, over the years we have spent a night at the Scanlon House B&B, two years at the Hilltop B&B, at least three years at the Cottage House Inn, and one year at the Stone Mill Inn.

Whatever the lodgings happen to be, the fall weekends in Lanesboro tend to take the same shape, year after year. We arrive at the Ladig residence at 9:30 a.m. just as Don is loading the bikes into their van. Fifteen minutes later we're entering the Dunn Brothers on Snelling and Grand to pick up some coffee and pastries. From there it's roughly a three-hour drive down Highway 52 through Cannon Falls, Rochester, Chatfield, and Fountain, to our destination.

We usually take the bike trail upstream that afternoon and downstream the next morning. The trail follows the Root River much of the way, with a few narrow canyons and quite a few bridges. I often make a suggestion before we head out: why not eat our picnic here in town; then we won't have to pack everything onto our bikes. This notion is invariably dismissed out of hand, and wisely so. It's not such a big deal to pack up our fixings, and it's always a pleasure to stop at a picnic table forty-five minutes up the trail, unfurl the India-print tapestry tablecloth that we're been using since our very first trip on the Luce Line more than three decades ago, and set out all the goodies. We used to make an effort to coordinate the menu, but now we just bring stuff—cheeses, salami, crackers, horseradish, cookies—confident that we'll cover most of the bases and no one will starve.

For our recent excursion Sherry booked two rooms at Mrs.B's, Lanesboro's oldest hotel, established in 1875. The layout of the building—its narrow hall, steep staircase, and smallish rooms—give you the impression that it's always been a hotel or a boarding house. Hilary and I ate there once many years ago, and since that time I've associated the place with ornate wallpaper, potpourris in every room, baskets full of yarn in every corner, and vintage needlework on the wall.

The building has changed hands at least three times since then, and the current owner, Trish, a middle-aged woman with seemingly boundless energy, has modernized it thoroughly while retaining just the right amount of "vintage" charm—very comfortable but not over-stuffed. In response to the pandemic, Trish has done all the cleaning and lowered her rates, and she no longer serves breakfast, which is also a plus in my opinion.

Two Audubon prints, expertly framed, hung from the wall of our second-story room. The single window, deep-set in the thick limestone walls, looked south down Main Street across the bike trail toward a canoe-rental outfit, the local historical museum, and, in the distance, the city park. Though small, it had a built-in electric fireplace wedged into a corner that you could "ignite" with a remote.

To my mind, the great challenge of the weekend would lie in finding something to do after dinner. On a normal trip we might sit around playing cards, drinking booze of various types, and (occasionally) trying to annoy one another with our falsetto Neil Young imitations. Then again, we might have gotten tickets to Commonwealth Theater, where we've seen quite a few plays together over the years, including the British comedy/romance, *Enchanted April*, Henrik Ibsen's last play, *When We the Dead Awaken*, and most memorably Tom Stoppard's *Arcadia*. The Covid virus rendered those indoor options unattractive or unavailable, but we devised perhaps an equally good one: sitting around a table on the patio behind the hotel thirty feet above the Root River with a half-full bottle of Grand Marnier that Sherry had brought along.

During the evening we continued to unwind the strands of conversations about family, music, food, and books that we'd initiated out on the trail, and started a few new ones, while wandering only occasionally into the world of politics, where we're all in perfect agreement about the deficiencies and dangers of the current administration.

There was no need to revive old standards like "Sugar Mountain" and "Cinnamon Girl": it was open-mike night in the parking lot behind the High Court Pub midway down the alley, with a live back-up band! The only song I recognized was "Johnny B. Goode," but the gathering was far enough away that it lent a pleasant background to our own conversation.

I remember a single starling squawking from a wire far about our heads in fading light, and, as darkness descended, a quarter-moon hung high in the sky to the south, with Jupiter and Saturn trailing behind it to the east. Just as we were getting up to go inside—yes, by that time the bottle was empty—a couple emerged from the darkness of the alley. It was Trish and her boyfriend, Greg, who had been playing in the band. We extended our compliments and they invited us to the house party taking place the next evening, giving us detailed instructions about how to get there. In the midst of their enthusiasm, I didn't have the heart to interrupt them with the news that we would be leaving town the next day.

The next morning was sunny, cool, and crisp, and Hilary and I sat on two Adirondack chairs on the sidewalk in front of the hotel, watching the world go by. Several livestock trucks passed by, and also a delivery truck with an enormous advertisement painted on the side for Kinky Blue and Pink liqueurs. Ugh. The driver made an impressive U-turn in the middle of the block—not much traffic at that time of day—and disappeared from sight into the loading dock of the liquor store.

A few minutes later a fit-looking retiree with a carefully groomed stubble took the chair next to mine. We talked about campgrounds—he owns a vintage Scamp—and about the hotels in Duluth. He told us that at one time he was part-owner of a sailing vessel docked at Indian Point, a mile or two up the St. Louis River from the harbor. "We would take it once a year up to Isle Royale, Thunder Bay, and beyond," he said.

"I take it you're not referring to just a thirty-foot craft," I said.

"Oh, no," he replied. "It was 150 feet long." And he went on to describe the sails and the rigging in some detail, using terminology most of which I was not familiar with.

"On its final voyage, some of the owners decided to sail it to England," he said. "They sailed too close to Greenland, got trapped in pack ice, and had to be rescued by a Danish shrimp boat. Our boat sank."

A few minutes later Don and Sherry appeared, well scrubbed and smiling, and we made our way on foot to the Home Sweet Home café at the other end of Main Street—that is to say, two blocks away. We ate an excellent breakfast al fresco and were soon on the trail again, chatting and pedaling. The morning was perfect for cycling, though the bike traffic was heavier than the previous afternoon.

The leaves were just beginning to turn, showing quite a bit of yellow but few reds beyond the low-lying tangles of sumac and Virginia creeper. We passed a gravel pit with some impressive piles of very fine sand, spotted a family sunbathing on the far side of the river, and also noticed an abandoned railroad bridge beyond a cornfield that looked worthy of further investigation on some future occasion.

Two hours and twenty miles later, we were back in town, saying our good-byes and hoisting our bikes onto our vehicles. An ice cream cone before departure? No. The line was too long.

Weekend with Vegetables

There are days in the life of a free lancer when he's just waiting for things: new chapter files, PDFs filled with proofer marks, images, proofs from the printer. Why not take the day off?

It seems sensible enough. And besides, there are always quite a few things that need to be done around the house: mow the lawn, take the vegetable scraps out to the compost pile, change a light bulb. Most important of all, perhaps, is to deal with those glorious tomatoes we brought home from the farmers' market on Sunday morning.

I had gotten an email from my friend Michel—a far better cook than I—mostly a photo of the spectacular tomatoes he'd gotten at the farmer's market. In response I sent him an old photo of my own.

"This is the perfect morning to head downtown," I wrote. "Here are a few heirloom tomatoes from our garden—the last two!"

The following email exchange ensued:

Michel: "Those look beautiful!"

Me: "And tasty! But this morning I'm thinking of baked leeks and squash with ground almonds. And I am literally stepping out the door as I write this."

Michel: "I find myself in a euphoric state when I go to the farmers market during the week, when it's not busy, and pick up bags of produce for a few dollars. I come home, lay them out on my table and want to take pictures of them or paint them, immortalize them ... cook them."

It was, indeed, a remarkable morning. The air was so fresh and cool that as we approached the stalls I said to Hilary, "I feel like I'm at the beach!" We bought so many things that we decided to carry our initial purchases back to the car and return for a second look around. At the very least, we still needed to pick up a bunch of cut flowers.

In the end, we brought home three robust bunches of leeks, a nice basket of six tomatoes, two huge red bell peppers (misshapen but still firm), a butternut squash, an acorn squash, a basket of potatoes, some fairly tough-looking green beans, a bunch of fresh basil the size of a bride's bouquet, and some fresh dill which was worth the price for the aroma alone.

The next day I used up half of the leeks and all the potatoes making a batch of the best potato-leek soup I've ever tasted.

We didn't have much of a chance to eat it, however. We'd been invited to Norton's annual Sukkoth party. (If we'd gone to the farmers' market a half-hour later, we would have met up with him buying a big bag of corn on the cob.)

I enjoy these parties, which are like a book convention, only smaller, and you know a lot more of the people. I relish the opportunity to reconnect with authors I got to know fairly well while working with them on their books, only to lose sight of them later—thoughtful, kind, and generous souls one and all.

A few old friends from the Bookmen years are also likely to be there. Brett Waldman and I discussed the best places to buy fresh fish in Bayfield, where he and his wife, Shiela, love to sail. He recommended a shop, practically across the street from the motel where we usually stay, that I've seen but never ventured into. And I had a good time with Bill Kaufmann reminiscing about shipping issues and the pleasures of lunchtime touch football. (Prior to his days with the lunchtime Bookmen football league, Bill was a star cornerback for the St. John's Johnies. His knees are still paying the price.)

Author John Coy and I discussed the fonts I used on a reprint of his book *Vroomaloom Zoom* back in 2010.

"Ah, yes, Croomby and Babelfish. I don't get much of an opportunity to use either of those nowadays."

John and I somehow got to talking about the Portuguese empire—he travels a lot—and when his wife, Fiona, joined us, we discussed the interview she did with essayist Geoff Dyer a few years back at the downtown library.

A few minutes later, Tom Pope was telling me about a book he's writing on screenwriting considered in the light of Aristotle's theory of *hamartia*. "You ought to read *Philosophy as Dramatic Theory* by the Spanish philosopher Julien Marias," I suggested.

"Who?" He replied. And he strode off to find a pen and a piece of paper.

Norton had grilled several planks of salmon for the event, and there were pots of ratatouille, bowls of pesto and spinach dip, corn on the cob, and three kinds of apple crisp at least.

But I especially enjoyed the time we spent with Norton's sister, Beverly, out on the screen porch. It had been decorated with a netting of corn-cobs, to serve as the tabernacle, and there, on a card table, sat the lemon, the palm leaf, the myrtle, and the willow. Beverly delivered the ritual Hebrew prayers in a powerful voice as she handled the plants one after another. I don't know what it all meant, but I was moved.

It wasn't until the next day that a bit more of the leek soup got eaten. But we'd been invited to a small retirement gathering that night for a friend at Ginger Hop. We filled up on spring rolls, calamari, and Jackie Chan burgers while Sheila, the guest of honor, told us about various things she'd received from colleagues at work, including a bottle of single malt scotch. We had soon hatched a plan for a Halloween poker game, with everyone arriving in kilts, drinking too much scotch, and watching Jackie Chan's masterpiece, *Rush Hour,* together.

All the while, the soup was doing just fine in the fridge. But by the next morning, the dill was shot, the basil had lost its glisten, and the tomatoes were starting to show their age—a few brownish patches on the skins. I was going to make spaghetti sauce and had gotten the onions going on the stove, but when I started to cut up the tomatoes it struck me that after removing the blemishes, they still looked (and tasted) quite good. Why turn them into a ho-hum pot of sauce?

The result of this dramatic about-face was a bowl of tomato-basil-garlic topping for toasted bread, commonly known as bruschetta. The word bruschetta refers to the bread, I believe, and I have a hunch there's an etymological connection between that word and the English word *brusque,* though I've never investigated.

It's a never-ending story. The butternut squash will go with the leeks in a melange, baked with heavy cream and topped with chopped almonds. The sun will continue to strike the dew on the grass, later there will be frost, you'll be able to see your breath. Orion will return, and the day will come when darkness arrives at four in the afternoon. You'll look down from the freeway overpass to see that the farmers' market, brightly lit under the snow-covered canopies, is filled with evergreen trees.

The Joy of Compost

Perhaps "joy" is too strong a word to describe the quiet pleasure one derives from a low mound of rotting leaves and vegetable scraps. Then again, must all our joys be feverish and exhausting?

The beauty of compost lies in the connections between the carrot peels we stuff into a clear plastic container by the sink, the leaves that enjoy a brief moment of glory before dropping every fall, and the rich dark organic matter that develops over time in the wire-enclosed bin in the far corner of the back yard.

I water the pile occasionally in dry weather, but I almost never climb inside the wire enclosure, which might be six feet in diameter, to turn the leaves and scraps. Mostly the pile takes care of itself, overfull by the time the snow falls, but sunken again soon enough after warm days return.

The lovely weather this fall made it easy to delay raking the leaves, and that presented an opportunity to extract the mature compost over several days, a few wheel barrel's full at a time. I dumped some on the tomato patch in the front yard by the driveway, and another good pile on the wedge-shaped plot of annuals near the front door. A few days later I brought some compost over to the terraced beds under the bedroom window, and I also spread some out around the turtleheads and the black-eyes susans.

None of this could really be called work. I spent a lot of time pondering garden strategy—far longer than I needed to.

One of the pleasures of the composting process is that it gets you out into the further reaches of the yard, places you wouldn't otherwise visit so often, thus giving you a fresh perspective on things you've looked at many times before. These are the moments when you begin to dimly comprehend how beautiful and precious life is, or can be, when things are going well and the weather's nice and you've got the time to zone out, attentive to the moss and the clouds and other things that mean nothing to you or anyone else—things quietly proceeding on their own paths.

Is compost really worth anything to the plants? I have read that it can improve soil structure, add nutrients, attract earthworms, and reduce problems with pests. I simply like the look of it. At this stage it's almost fluffy, but by next spring the brown clumps of matter will have flattened out and disappeared. Perhaps I'll even have forgotten I ever messed with them, as the violets and bleeding-heart emerge and a new pile of leaves, compressed by the snow, sinks down by infinitesimal degrees ever further in its misshapen wire bin.

Halcyon Days

The word for these golden fall days is "halcyon." The colors of the changing leaves are magnificent and the temperature is perfect—low sixties creeping improbably into the seventies from time to time, with even cooler nights.

Yes, but how are we to respond? Each moment is perfection in itself. Why do anything? But we *must* do something. It's the motive for and definition of poetry: the intensification and exaltation of experience.

I'm not a poet, so I spent the day Thursday repairing and regrading the window-well behind the yew bushes just outside our living room windows. All the while, I was thinking to myself, "I should be reading Sir Thomas Browne's *Religio Medici*." But first things first.

I dug out five inches of soil from the well while lying on my stomach behind the bushes and replaced it with two bags of cherry stone pebbles, wondering as I did so if anyone really appreciates how beautiful cherry stone pebbles are. I used the excavated dirt to shape the drainage away from the house, topped that with a sheet of landscape fabric and a few bags of cypress mulch, and had a lightning flash of intuition that sent me back to Home Depot to buy a five-foot piece of drain pipe to extend the nearby downspout out beyond the roots of the shrubs into the yard.

The weather the next day was so inviting that Hilary and I drove down to Rice Lake State Park, one of the least celebrated parks in the state, though it's a mere ninety minutes from the Twin Cities. We camped, we hiked the perimeter of the park, past golden leaves and cattails rustling in the gusty wind. We ate chips and bean dip for dinner, washed it down with a bit of bad sauvignon blanc, then sat on our indispensable camp chairs looking up at the brilliant stars through the naked branches overhead, which were faintly lit by the flickering campfire. The Orionid Meteor Show was at its peak, but we saw nothing along those lines.

The next morning I was awakened by a flash of lighting, or the headlights of a car passing by on the gravel loop road around the campsite. Thunder a few seconds later, then the rain arrived. Ten flurried minutes later we were all packed up and snug inside the car, only half soaked ourselves, headed for Owatonna in the dark with the smell of wet manure from the nearby farm fields coursing through our nostrils.

We ate breakfast at The Kitchen in downtown Owatonna, bought a pumpkin in near-darkness at the farmers' market in the town square, and stopped for another cup of coffee at a place called Goodbye Blue Monday Coffee House in downtown Northfield.

The place was bubbling with activity. A large group of men sat around a long table near the front window. Closer to us, five young women were discussing an event they had all attended the previous evening, though I never gleaned what it was. The street outside was still fairly dark, but the long warm room inside was well-lit, colorful, and filled with animated chatter—a sort of ideal vision of funky intellectual stimulation and collegial *gemütlichkeit*.

I was only a little disappointed to discover that the women behind me were discussing, not Hegelian dialectic or even the novels of Doris Lessing, but their pets. One of them was trying to find someone, without quite asking outright, who would agree to give her "million dollar cat" shots twice a day while she was gone on a four-day trip to Madison. There were no takers.

Northfield was hosting its annual art crawl that morning; before we left the house I had printed out a map pinpointing the participating galleries and studios. But the event wasn't set to open until ten, and by that time we were back home again, sitting comfortably in front of another, more robust, fire. It was still drizzling, but I was pleased to note that not a single drop had penetrated the window well in the basement.

In the midst of this pleasant *hygge* (pronounced "hoo-ga," I'm told), I turned, finally, to *Religio Medici* by Sir Thomas Browne, the English essayist whom I had been eager to get a handle on for some time.

[Music] unties the ligaments of my frame, takes me to pieces, dilates me out of myself, and by degrees, mee thinks, resolves me into heaven.

Yes, music. I fetched my twelve-CD collection of the keyboard works of William Byrd, a composer Browne himself might have listened to. Upon first listen, years ago, I got the impression that this set was actually composed of a single CD reproduced twelve times. I am now convinced that a harpsichord doesn't sound exactly like a virginal or a muselar. There's a good deal of exploring still to do here. Meanwhile:

I love to lose myself in a mystery, to pursue my reason to an "o altitudo." 'Tis my solitary recreation to pose my apprehension with those involved enigmas and riddles of the Trinity, with Incarnation and Resurection. I can answer all the objections of Satan, and my rebellious reason, with that odd resolution I learned from Tertullian, "Certum est quia impossible est."

Browne is sometimes referred to as an English Montaigne, but that French skeptic fueled his reflections on Horace and Ovid, while Browne seems more concerned to reconcile Christian doctrine with human reason, or at least to conjecture how much of experience lies beyond reason's purview.

The two writers share an easy command of prose, always curious, often bemused, never strident. Browne is credited with adding more than a hundred new words to the English language that are still in use. Quite a few of his neologisms have since vanished from the lexicon, too, hence the need for the lengthy but easy-to-use set of notes in the back, which help us to figure what, for example, *dissentaneous* and *improperations* mean.

One of Browne's favorite words is *indifference*, which he uses to describe, not the attitude we might have toward an idea or thing, but a point or issue that is not so important as to demand our assent. An indifference is a position that we can take or leave to suit our whimsy, or suspend judgment on altogether, entertaining it, as it were, while neither condemning it nor embracing it wholeheartedly.

I can see why the term never caught on, though it seems to be a seventeenth century equivalent of our own "whatever," or that immortal colloquialism we use to describe contending views that aren't really as rigorously opposed as we're being asked to believe: "Same difference."

Second Summer

I t was one of those stunning mornings after an overnight rain, cool and wet and bright with sun. Yellow leaves on the trees, tending toward orange-red here and there.

I had gone to pick up some vegetables for soup and other concoctions; the store was largely deserted, a seminar was underway in the produce department, and I thought to myself: "That's what I should have been: a produce stocker."

For a split second I even entertained the thought that maybe it wasn't too late! No, it is too late.

When I stepped out into the glaring sun of the parking lot, I was pleasantly reminded of a parking lot I crossed in Apache Junction, Arizona, many years ago on a similarly brilliant morning. There was a cactus wren hopping around amid the litter that morning, and there might even have been frost on the concrete. But the essential quality was unbounded light and joy. Just like yesterday. And today.

How do we explain this flashback? It might have been because I was listening to a Carlos Nakai CD on my way to the store. Why? Because I'm getting a string of digital images together for a talk I'm scheduled to give on Friday about the National Parks. Earlier in the morning I'd been sorting through a few scenes of Canyonlands.

No point in talking about the Maze. Few in the audience

of fifty-odd retirees are likely to be going there any time soon. But what about Horseshoe Canyon, with its spooky Barrier-style petroglyphs? It's a seven-mile hike there and back down the floor of a deserted canyon, but nevertheless it would be well worth showing some images of the art.

I had planned to cook up some broccoli-wild rice casserole for my in-laws, but in the end I decided to make a batch of what I call Beltrami Salad.

Count Beltrami, as you may know, was an Italian adventurer (but not a count) who hooked a ride on a steamboat with U.S. Army explorer Stephen Long in 1823 up the Minnesota River, then down the Red River of the North. Long had been sent to determine where the border between the United States and British territories lay; Beltrami was confident that he was about to discover the source of the Mississippi River through the back door, as it were. Upon reaching the Red Lake River, he hired an Ojibwe guide and headed upstream. The guide abandoned him soon afterward, but Beltrami persevered, paddling and hauling his canoe upstream single-handedly, and he eventually arrived at a body of water he named Lake Luisa, in honor of his girlfriend.

It isn't the headwaters of the Mississippi, but there's a monument on a hill above the highway nearby commemorating Beltrami's near-miss.

Beltrami Salad is part Italian and part Native American. It consists of wild rice mixed with orzo and flavored with sautéed shallots and tarragon—a bit of a French touch. There were some mushrooms in the fridge getting old, and I cooked some of them up, too, and tossed them in.

The smell of wild rice cooking reminds me of wet tree bark—a woodsy, autumnal smell. Hilary brought in a handful of parsley from the front garden, and I tossed that in, too.

The day had remained stunning throughout, but as twilight approached I was looking around for something suitable to read—something to sustain the pastoral yet vaguely ecstatic mood. I finally hit upon *Good Seeds—A Menominee Indian Food Memoir* by Thomas Pecore Weso.

In this short book, hardly more than a hundred pages long, Weso describes growing up on the Menominee Reservation, his focus being on the things he hunted, the crops he and his relatives grew, and the berries and nuts various members of the tribe gathered. The book has a quiet tone, direct, honest, charming, and curious rather than edgy or strident. The first two chapters set the mood, with grandmother cooking downstairs while grandfather prays—or "dreams," as Weso puts it—upstairs. Subsequent chapters are devoted to fishing, hunting, and fruit-gathering, though there are also chapters about German beer and Wisconsin Diner food. Each chapter concludes with a few recipes.

Weso's grandfather looms large in the early pages. He comes across as a leader, a diplomat, someone not only capable of building bridges between whites and Indians, but also aware of how important it is to do so. Weso reports that he was thirty-five years old the first time he saw his grandfather in traditional Indian garb. It was at a peyote ceremony of the Native American church. His grandfather was wearing a headband more intricate and idiosyncratic than any he had seen before, and he speculated that it dated from pre-contact times. He considers it a reflection of how highly esteemed in the community his grandfather was.

"I can now see," Weso writes, "that Grandpa was trying to create a political climate in accordance with a spiritual climate, and I think people expected him to do this in his role as a medicine man. My grandfather talked to white people, black people, Indian people, and he tried to learn how to interact with each equally ... My grandfather never told boastful stories about himself, as he was very modest, but he was a leader."

Probing a little deeper into his grandfather's philosophy, Weso concludes that it was based on the urge to help people feel better about themselves. "If people feel good about themselves, they take better care of themselves, their domain, their town, and their land."

The good-natured tone of *Good Seeds* is no doubt a reflection of Weso's success at absorbing the teachings of his revered grandfather, from whom he learned that even the simplest daily tasks could carry far more than a merely practical import.

"Part of Grandpa's teaching was gardening. We always had a family garden. If any of us went to the garden to do some watering or hoeing, we could see our efforts bear fruit. That reward also had a spiritual aspect."

Good Seeds isn't a self-help book, however, and once having introduced us to this philosophy, Weso proceeds to describe various food-related activities on the reservation that he thinks might interest his readers. Here are a few typical remarks:

> When I was young, I thought a deer was a big animal, but it is not, especially on the reservation. A deer is really a big rabbit. It is tasty, and if a deer is available, it is welcome. Venison stew tastes delicious. But comparatively, it is the runty ungulate after bison, then elk. There was this guy on the rez with a huge appetite who could sit down and eat an entire deer. People did not like hunting with him.

Bears are another source of meat on the Menominee rez, but I was never much of a bear hunter. I was a good shot, and I did not mind killing a squirrel, a rabbit, or a partridge. Even if it had a soul, it could not be a very big soul. I could not, however, bring myself to kill bear. I did kill one as a young man, and that was enough. It was like killing another man.

Any time a group of people live together, suddenly there is no firewood within walking distance.

The body of a beaver is about the size of the body of a white-tail deer ... Some people like the taste of beaver, but to me it is less desirable—though it does taste better than muskrat or raccoon."

On the rez are many edible ferns. Fiddleheads, curled-up shoots of ferns, are not that delicious. They are slimy, mucilaginous, and furry. The ostrich fiddle- head fern is edible—not poisonous. I could not eat a pot full.

Generally blackberries grow where bears live, and there are mosquitoes. All in all, the mosquitoes are worse than the bears.

I was surprised to learn that in his youth, Weso was influenced by the writings of Euell Gibbons, like many other outdoorsy types, including me. "I was from that generation," he says. At another point he writes, with both humor and candor:

This was during President Lyndon Johnson's Great Society, the era when people were expressing their cultural heritage more readily. Headbands had become a common thing. Anyone with one recessive Indian gene wore a headband. Those were the days when I always had a pair of moccasins. From early spring to late fall, I wore only moccasins, not as an expression of culture, but because they were very comfortable.

The portrait he paints of reservation life is relaxed and multifaceted. His grandmother, who also looms large throughout the book, worked in a store from six-thirty a.m. till dark, and often served canned sauerkraut at the dinner table. Though she sometimes reminisced about traditional foraging techniques, she was not nostalgic for those days.

She would say, Do you want to live in a tipi? Do you want to spend most of the day bringing wood home so you don't freeze to death? Yes, it sounds great, but do you want to do that? Do you want to chase a big animal with a spear?

In the last two chapters, Weso returns to the family and community life of the reservation, the local fair, the pow-wow, and the challenges of food storage when serving ten or twenty hungry people daily. In the final chapter he even describes the malevolent spirits that danced on the walls and seemed to live in the furnace room of the family home, which had previously been a jail. He speaks fondly of photos taken of himself outside the house as a young boy, sitting on horseback with Hopalong Cassidy six-shooters hanging from his belt—a gift from his uncle Billy, who was as near to being a father as anyone was. Several times he mentions in passing "when my uncle Billy was murdered" but doesn't elaborate, and it gives an unsettling twist to the notion of "spirit" that has carried us through this generally low-key, heartily sincere, and often delightful book.

Killing Time in St. Paul

It was a retirement party in a neighborhood without a name on the eastern edge of Highland Park in St. Paul. I dropped Hilary off—she was one of the organizers—and puttered north on Hamline Avenue past Randolph and St. Clair to Grand Avenue. On the CD player, alto saxophonist Frank Morgan was spinning an energetic version of Charlie Parker's "Now's the Time." Indeed.

I had ninety minutes to kill before the event got underway, and I had a plan. First stop, Kowalski's Market: low light and dazzling displays everywhere, many types of "artisanal" crackers at $6.50 a box. I noticed that the display sign for one regional brand, Maple Terroir, had been misspelled as Maple Terrior. People in St. Paul do love their dogs, but all the same, I thought I ought to tell someone.

There was no one in the booth, so I mentioned the goof to a passing woman wearing an apron, and she seemed pleased. "Oh, you must be an English major," she said with a big smile. It's been a long time since anyone took an interest in what my college major was! No. I shook my head. "...but I do edit books for a living." Not exactly true, but the woman looked as pleased as punch. I think I might have made her day.

My "plan" was a simple one: to pick up a box of Wasa crisps. They're sold in France under the name Cracottes; that's how Hilary and I first ran into them and how we refer to them to this day. Old habits die hard, and in any case, the word Wasa connotes those puffy but thick and hard crackers that are difficult to bite through and actually taste and smell like the farm. Cracottes, on the other hand, are airy and light—the perfect vehicle to carry slices of hard-boiled egg with wasabi mayonnaise on a bed of fresh arugula to your mouth.

I wandered the store with my single item (net weight 4.9 ounces) dangling in a green plastic basket, feeling a little foolish as I watched people ordering quart containers of delightful looking salads from the deli. I briefly admired a sheet cake with a splendid rendering of Mt. Rushmore on top. I pondered the fresh fish sitting in beds of ice in a glass-fronted gondola, took in the strange aromas of fancy soaps in the cleaning aisle, and eventually added a box of Kind Bars (net weight 5.2 ounces) to my stash. Why? I don't know. I haven't eaten one of those since the Luminary Loppet of 2016, where they were being given away out on the ice on Lake of the Isles.

Kowalski's doesn't have a self-check. I thought I'd found one, but it turned out I was standing behind an unoccupied cash register. The entry pad was incomprehensible, and nothing was lighting up. The woman at the customer service desk saw me, took pity, and called me over to her counter.

Finally back on the street with my purchases, I headed west on Grand Avenue a half-block to Sixth Chamber Books. I seldom visit bookstores these days—I already have quite a few books—but I'd been reading Dante's *Divine Comedy* and thought I might come across a mentor paperback edition of the Ciardi translation of the *Paradiso*.

Besides, I still had forty-five minutes to kill.

I had no luck with the Dante, but ended up purchasing two

books from the memoir section, *Kafka Was the Rage: a Greenwich Village Memoir* by Anatole Broyard, and *Finding Fontainebleau: an American Boy in France* by Thad Carhart. (Carhart's other book, *The Little Piano Shop on the Left Bank,* is wonderful.)

I think of Broyard as the Adam Gopnik of an earlier era. Both were from French or quasi-French New World cities (New Orleans and Montreal, respectively); both fell in love with New York, had small, seedy apartments, studied art history with famous critics, had plenty of bohemian adventures, and read a lot of books.

Broyard made some money while in the service during the war, and among the first adventures he describes is opening a used bookshop in Greenwich Village.

I had imagined myself like Saint Jerome in his study [he writes] *bent over his books, with the tamed lion of his conquered restlessness at his feet. My customers would come and go in studious silence, pausing, with averted eyes, to leave the money on my desk. But it didn't turn out like that. What I hadn't realized was that, for many people, a bookshop is a place of last resort, a kind of moral flophouse. Many of my customers were the kind of people who go into a bookshop when all other diversions have failed them. Those who had no friends, no pleasures, no resources came to me. They came to read the handwriting on the wall, the bad news. They studied the shelves like people reading the names on a war memorial.*

Others came, Broyard discovered, not to buy books but to tell their stories.

It was the talkers who gave me the most trouble. Like the people who had sold me books, the talkers wanted to sell me their lives, their fictions about themselves, their philosophies. Following the example of the authors on the shelves, infected perhaps by them, they told me of their families, their love affairs, their illusions and disillusionments. I was indignant. I wanted to say, Wait a minute! I've already got stories here! Take a look at those shelves!

While I pretended to listen, I asked myself which were more real—theirs, or the stories on the shelves ... In the commonplaceness of their narratives, some of these talkers anticipated the direction that American fiction would eventually take—away from the heroic, the larger than life, toward the ordinary, the smaller than life.

These excerpts may sound a little grim, but the tone of the narrative is consistently crisp and often funny. In one brief semi-Freudian episode, for example, Broyard inadvertently destroys several corkscrews while trying to open a bottle of wine in Anaïs Nin's apartment. Just standing there in the bookstore aisle, I got a renewed sense of Broyard's buoyant and incisive prose, which I dimly recalled from his book reviews in the *Times*, but I hesitated before making my way to the front desk with the volume. Then it occurred to me that it cost only 25 cents more than the Kind Bars waiting for me in the car. And the woman behind the counter had let me use the restroom. Let's give her some custom.

"The owners are here most days," she told me as she was ringing me up.

"I live in Golden Valley," I said. "I rarely get over to this part of town."

"They also keep a record of their stock online, so you should check the website if you don't find what you're looking for. They also run a shop in River Falls."

"I think I've been to that shop," I said. "I got a copy of volume one of Walter Benjamin's collected works out there. Are you familiar with his work?"

"I've never heard of him."

"Well, I wouldn't recommend him."

Back in the car, I took the first left turn off Grand, and then a strange thing happened. I thought I was on Hamline, which I was not. I was planning to turn left on Hartford, which would have been a mistake. In any case, every left turn seemed to go immediately down a hill into the woods, which was very odd. When I finally looked at the signs, I discovered that I was at the corner of Edgecumbe Drive and Ford Parkway, which seemed impossible. (Nice neighborhood, though.)

Curling west back to familiar territory on Snelling Avenue, I made my way easily to the house, just in time to take a look at Celeste's hand-made books (a head start on one of her retirement projects) before the guests arrived, and to pour champagne, both white and pink, into an array of tall thin glasses of various sizes and shapes.

Let the party begin!

Snow Approaches

It's one of those exciting days known only to people of the north. Snow is on the way! Not a disaster. Just a fact. Whether it will be eight inches or two, it will be here tomorrow, which makes today a sort of temporal enclosure or envelope, a span within which to get a few things done and savor the tag end of the fall season.

These things include:

a) finally raking the back yard. This is easy. What with the woods and the garden, there isn't much left to rake. And I've already run the mower over the leaves once or twice.

b) getting out the ladder and cutting off the dead branch on the mulberry tree that's been fully visible out the bedroom window, bent at a grotesque angle, for the last two years. Something about using one of those saws on the end of a long metal pole is unusually tiring. I think it may be the work involve. But it's fun to be out in that part of the yard, where I seldom go. And looking around the corner of the house to see how the *viburnum trilobum* we planted this summer is doing, I see that two "volunteer" Norway maples have sprouted in the vicinity.

The fall leaf color was spectacular this year, and nothing surpassed the noble, buttery yellow of the Norway maples. They're considered an invasive species, I know, but I find that judgment ridiculous: You could let one grow for five years and remove it in five minutes. So what's the problem? My thought is to cut down the entire mulberry tree and see what these two maples can do. But we'll leave that project for the spring.

c) putting sunflower seeds in the feeders. This may sound like a recurring chore, but the raccoons have been raiding our feeder repeatedly and we'd gotten into the habit of leaving them empty or depositing only a handful of seed at a time. Perhaps the raccoons are gone by now?

I took a look out the window half an hour later and noticed that a nuthatch, a chickadee, and a red-bellied woodpecker were all feeding, with a goldfinch swinging merrily from the finch feeder hanging below. I spotted a hairy woodpecker on the trunk of the silver maple and a junco in the underbrush. Now, there's a winter bird for you, though it seems the juncos mostly pass through on either end of the season.

d) bringing in the garden hoses and shutting off the water. While out in the garden I noticed that one day lily was still "in bloom." Perhaps it's frozen. The purple lamium is also blooming. And the broad, elephant-eared leaves of the Siberian bugloss are still dark green. I didn't realize we had so many.

e) bringing the wrought-iron chairs in from the deck. The three thoughts that accompany this chore are 1). Don't fall down the basement stairs; 2). I should clear the ashes out of the grill; 3). We could grill something tonight!

f) wrapping the cedar trees with green plastic fencing to keep the deer that come up from Bassett Creek at bay.

I cleared the leaves out of the gutters a few days ago, surprising though it may seem. It strikes me that this is a senseless task—almost a superstition. The gutters are frozen all winter, so what difference does it make if they have leaves in them?

At long last, the ladder and the pole saw go back into the garage, along with the rake and the broom Hilary used to sweep off the deck. It remains to saw up the mulberry branch, but that can wait for an hour or two.

There's a pot of day-old vegetable soup in the refrigerator. And now I see a downy woodpecker climbing the half-dead tree outside the window.

Once the chores are done, the still relatively balmy afternoon (35 degrees) calls out for a field trip of some kind. So we drove across the Mississippi to the Banfill-Locke Art Center in Fridley where the paintings of the Swedish-American painter Elof Wedin are on display. It's a nice gallery housed in a white frame, two-story building that dates to 1847. It was once an inn catering to drovers on the Red River oxcart trail. Rice Creek meanders down to the Mississippi through a park north of the building.

Wedin's paintings are interesting, though I prefer his WPA style to his later, more angular and abstract 1950s style. Hilary chatted at some length with one of the volunteers while I ate crackers and nuts—it was the opening—and circulated again and again through the four rooms of the exhibit, finding the paintings more interesting with every pass.

It took about a day for the ox cart drivers of the 1850s to get to downtown Minneapolis from Banfill-Locke. It took us fifteen minutes to get to the Northern Clay Center in the Seward neighborhood, south of downtown, where a show of award-winning Canadian pottery was on display. For my money, the functional pottery for sale in the gallery was far more interesting, and infinitely more affordable, than the items on display in the exhibition hall. Many of the names are familiar—Cuellar, Swanson, Norman, Severson—but the pots remain diverse and appealing. One potter from Superior, Wisconsin, whose name I forget, had four massive yet handsome jugs on display. I kept trying to imagine what I'd put in one of them, if I bought it: Orzo? Quinoa? Coffee beans?

A few blocks down Franklin Avenue Hilary spotted a sign halfway up a side street that said Boneshaker Books. We circled the block, parked, and went in.

It's a nifty little bookshop with a radical tinge, about the size of a farmhouse kitchen. Three bearded youths were reading at scattered chairs. Two twenty-somethings sat behind the checkout counter. There were plenty of chapbooks, zines, and small-press items on the rack. And I noticed that the section called "literature" was hardly bigger than the one called "anarchism."

I'm all in favor of anarchism myself—just so long as everyone behaves themselves.

The great thing about small bookstores is that they expose you to new things without overwhelming you with options. I saw one interesting book called *Utopia or Bust: a Guide to the Present Crisis* by Benjamin Kunkel. Better yet, Hilary spotted a book called *Why New Orleans Matters* on the "used" shelf for a dollar.

Back to the Garden

Sometimes it's a good idea to step back from the news for a while. There will always be more. And it will rarely be good.

The other day I pulled a book called *Back to the Garden* off the shelf and retreated all the way back to the Paleolithic. The author, James McGregor, is evidently an expert on the relations between cities and their surrounding landscape, but in this book he's less interested in aesthetics than in agriculture. Yet the title might well make us suspicious. We all know we've got to get back to the garden. Didn't Crosby, Stills, Nash and Young tell us as much at the end of "Woodstock" and follow that exhortation up with some evocative high-pitched shouts? Perhaps McGovern is offering us here yet one more serving of bucolic fantasy, exploring the prehistoric past in an effort to locate precisely where human civilization went wrong and offering advice as to how we can return to the life of semi-egalitarian bliss in the midst of field and forest.

No. The book is a lot more interesting than that. McGregor has an image in mind—he calls it First Nature— of a balanced relationship between urban and rural activities, and he suggests that we've lost sight of that balance. In his view, we lost it fairly recently. To prove his point, he reexamines almost the entire history of civilization, going all the way back to the Stone Age in search of clues about how and why changes in food production came about. For the most part he spares us the cautionary lectures, focusing on the facts while challenging quite a few of the theories that have been constructed around them by anthropologists and ecologists. In fact, McGregor is so wedded to the evidence that after mentioning his First Nature paradigm in the introduction, he doesn't bring it up again for almost a hundred pages.

In the mean time, McGregor spins a series of scholarly narratives about, for example, what the archeological record at Jericho, Abu Hureyra, and Çatalhöyük tell us about how farming developed. He rejects the theory that centralized power and vast irrigation systems lie at the heart of the story, arguing instead that small-scale floodwater farming played the crucial role. He also highlights the significance of cultures in the Danube Valley and the Hungarian Plain that flourished between 5000 and 3500 BCE, which he refers to as Old Europe. I'd never heard of it.

Carrying the point one step farther, McGregor asserts that our widespread misunderstanding of the process by which farming developed reflects biases ingrained in nineteenth century historiography. In his view, the narrative of state formation, which was a major political preoccupation of post-Napoleonic Europe, was further linked with the origins of the coercive power of the community—that is to say, with the origins of war. For theorists imbued with the thought of that era, three distinct theoretical concerns were inextricably blended together: the history of cultivation and domestication, the rise of the nation-state, and the story of warfare. Although these movements are distinct and only marginally congruent, nineteenth-century historiography joined them in a way that contemporary theorists must struggle to undo. The archaeological record suggests that the agricultural revolution, far from being the product of a single powerful civilization, was an accumulation of scattered practical insights bundled into an ensemble of seeds, herds, and cultivation techniques that was adapted to a variety of cultures and habitats.

McGregor soberly examines the nutritional theories of those who argue that the introduction of grains into the diet was a mistake, finding the Neolithic revolution to be a mixed bag. People lived longer, and the landscape could support more of them, but they also suffered more often from diseases. He finds the evidence in support of an early matriarchal culture that was shattered by violent invasion to be inconclusive at best. Once again, contemporary political agendas are likely being projected onto the distant past.

A third popular argument that McGregor questions is the one that sets wilderness as a model against which to measure the ravages of civilization. He writes:

> *Heretical or not, there are good reasons to reject wilderness as the poster child for biological life. This is not to reject wilderness itself but only to reject its role as stand-in for the whole of nature. If we ask ourselves whether the wilderness concept, during its two-century reign, has done a good job of standing up for the natural world, the answer has to be a resounding "No!" During that short time, more damage has been done to the landscape than ever before in human history.*

McGregor thinks he knows the reason why: the concept of wilderness was the creation, not of biologists or ecologists, but of poets and philosophers. Man has no place in wilderness, by definition, except as an occasional guest. It cannot be improved upon. At best, it can be preserved, untouched.

One of my favorite sections focuses on water use practices in Libya during the Roman era. In those days North Africa (along with Sicily and Egypt) was the breadbasket of the Empire. Conventional wisdom has it that the Romans abused the environment, extracting from it whatever they could get to feed its urban population while leaving behind a desert wasteland that has never recovered.

According to McGregor, the evidence doesn't support that view. Almost the reverse. Archeologists have found olive presses throughout North Africa, and experts estimate its annual export of oil to Rome might have approached a million liters. How was this possible? It was due to a meticulous engineering of the seasonal rainfall through the *wadis*, which allowed farmers to increase their yields considerably and devote some of their attention to cash crops. But it required diligence to operate the dams, catch-basins, and canals and keep them in working order. Thus the conventional theory that intensive cultivation lead to desertification must be scrapped. McGregor writes:

> *Intensive agriculture [in Libya] led to soil enrichment, not depletion...Roman North Africa did not fail in its job of producing food for the regional market. Just the opposite occurred: an international market failure brought on by invasion and fragmentation within the Roman Empire made export-based agriculture unsustainable. Political change, not environmental irresponsibility, led to the abandonment of productive infrastructure in North Africa.*

I have been emphasizing here a few of the unorthodox positions that McGregor advances in the course of his ramble through history, but the greater part of the book consists of the historical material itself, which McGregor presents in a clear, studied, low-key tone that makes for easy reading. His interests range from the cave paintings of the Paleolithic to the romantic theories of Goethe and Kant, from the conflicting philosophies of Empedocles and Parmenides to the physiocratic theories of the Enlightenment.

But whatever the subject may be, it will turn out to having a bearing on how we treat the environment as we produce food. For example, in his analysis of Adam Smith's *Wealth of Nations*, McGregor draws our attention to the central role played by money as the medium through which the "invisible hand" does its work. We take that for granted, without considering that when the theory was formulated, it left out the world of agricultural exchange almost entirely.

> *Historically [he writes] the universal use of money and the acceptance of exchange value over intrinsic value required substantial intellectual adjustment and often wrenching social change. It is no accident that the seminal eighteenth-century theorist of money was not a Frenchman but a Scot.*

In light of McGregor's curious and even-tempered approach to his subjects, it should come as no surprise that his concluding remarks lack apocalyptic fervor. Having spread before us a rich tapestry of ideas and practices, it only remains to connect the dots.

> *Massive government subsidies, indirect benefits in the form of infrastructure, and protective isolation from liability and health-related costs make contemporary agriculture economically viable. The cost of addressing the obesity that modern crops create would itself be sufficient to tip the balance in favor of ecologically sound practices.*

Ain't it the truth! Yet a more insistent advocate for change might have inserted the word "only" so that the sentence reads "ONLY massive government subsidies ... make contemporary agriculture economically viable."

One advantage of taking such a long view of the subject is that it allows McGregor to assert with confidence that our current agricultural practices may be considered as merely a "bubble"—albeit a two-hundred year bubble—in an otherwise largely successful attempts to produce ample food without undermining the long-term prospects of continuing to do so. I'm not so sure about that myself. But to my mind, what makes McGregor's history so interesting isn't the conclusions he arrives at so much as the way-stations we visit as we follow its wandering path, from Bronze Age shipbuilding techniques to rice cultivation in the Po Valley to the Marshall Plan. It's a miniature Enlightenment compendium on the order of the Abbé Raynal's *History of the Two Indies*, inspired by a rational concept of husbandry guided by past experience and an underlying concern for long-term sustainability.

The loftiness of McGregor's perspective has its virtues, but after finishing the book, I felt that I'd hardly gotten my hands dirty. It also occurred to me that he's overlooked two factors that have played a large role in the development of modern agribusiness. First of all, farming is hard work, and most people don't want to do it. I was at a conference not long ago and in the course of chatting with a sales rep I learned that he grew up on a farm near Lamberton along with twelve siblings.

"How many of them are still in farming?" I asked.

"None," he replied.

Second, as population continues to rise worldwide, here are a lot more mouths to feed than there were a hundred years ago. Yet most people either can't or don't want to pay a large portion of their income for expensive, ecologically sustainable food.

While I'm at it, let me add a third caveat: Although McGregor draws a number of general conclusions about agriculture near the end of the book, his focus throughout has been the Mediterranean landscape. And it's a lot easier to generate enthusiasm, both practical and aesthetic, for gentle hills laced with ancient stone walls and planted in grapes, olives, artichokes, and wheat, than for monotonous expanses of corn and soybeans that will never appear on a dining room table anywhere on earth.

Near the end of the book, McGregor writes:

> *Understanding traditional farming would anchor a shift in values. This shift needs to begin with an appreciation of the history of food and its culture, of the land that produces the food, of the men and women who care for the land and for what it yields.*

I doubt whether the author was thinking about the Latino workers of California's Central Valley when he wrote those words, though they are the workers we depend upon for our carrots and broccoli. It's more likely he was envisioning the sort of small-scale family-run operation that supports a chicken coop and dairy cows, pasturage, and a wide array of farm-to-market crops to keep itself afloat. It's an attractive vision, and not that far removed from the farms the Roman polymath Varro described in *Rerum Rusticarum Libri Tres* back in 37 BC. One big difference is worth mentioning, I think: the farms of Roman times were worked mostly by slaves and "hands." Cato the Elder, in his treatise on farming, recommends that the estate manager buy his workers a new cloak once every two years, and also advises him to sell off his old oxen and injured slaves every autumn.

Ending his long investigation on a hopeful note, McGregor suggests that the shift in values he refers to might already be underway. Here he seems to be a little behind the times. He refers to "the growth and spread of slow food restaurants, edible landscaping, community gardens and backyard gardening, community-supported agriculture, farmers' markets, and local-food consumerism." It seems to me the shift in values that underlies those movements is well underway. Yet even today, less than one percent of farmland in the United States is given over to organic farming.

After finishing *Back to the Garden*, I headed to the basement to hunt up an old copy *of Gaining Ground: the Renewal of America's Small Farms*, which came out 35 years ago. No luck. Then I turned to another classic close at hand, *The Country and the City* by Raymond Williams, but I could tell almost immediately that its focus—literary rather than practical—wasn't right for the occasion. Finally I settled on "The Making of a Marginal Farm," a piece from Wendell Berry's *Recollected Essays*, to summon the smell of manure, the satisfaction of working hard and eating home-grown vegetables, and the almost metaphysical bond that develops between the farmer and his or her animals, fields, and broader community. Would it have been beside the point for Berry to mentioned that being poor is also part of the equation?

November – National Poetry Month

National poetry month? I know what you're going to say. Fake news!

In fact, I'm simply making a modest proposal that poetry month be shifted from April, when there's already a good deal of poetry in the air, to November, when we could actually use a few blasts of it from the printed page.

New books of poetry appear in significant numbers at this time of year, their authors (and publishers) hoping for sales from shoppers looking for something light and relatively inexpensive to get for Aunt Tillie, who is never going to make her way through the new biography of U. S. Grant, though she might enjoy the crisp and enigmatic new collection by Michael Dennis Browne.

I'm not trying to suggest that poetry is invariably sweet, frivolous, and inconsequential. More often people complain that poetry is unnecessarily difficult and bewildering. I would argue that whatever else it is, poetry is of the essence of life. It is never theoretical, never political, always actual. Description becomes speech, thought becomes drama. The unstated punch-line of every poem is something on the order of "Well I'll be darned!" or "Who would have thought it?"

There are times, however, when the latent drama of poetry is difficult to summons. The words lie flat, the rhythm eludes us, we're wondering what the "point" is. November is also a time of poetry readings, as authors set up events to promote their new works. (Christmas is coming.)

Hilary and I attended several last week. On Monday Michael Dennis Browne read at Magers & Quinn from *Chimes*, his new collection of shorter poems. "I am a happy man tonight," he said, and it was easy to see why. His children were there, including his son, who flew in from California as a surprise. There were old friends like Louis Jenkins and Norita Dittberner-Jax, and new collaborators like composer David Evan Thomas and Nodin Press publisher Norton Stillman.

Michael told us stories about his father and mother— stories you won't find in the book. The poems in the collection are drawn from every phase in his career, and Michael was clearly relishing the return journey, though he also read one more recent bitter-sweet poem in which he imagines his family sitting around the fire at the cabin once he's gone.

A few days later we stopped in at Common Good Books to hear a trio of poets—Joyce Sutphen, Tim Nolan, and Sharon Chmielarz—read from their books. Their styles could not have been more different. Joyce has a twinkly eye and a slow, soft delivery, Tim used the blunt comedic approach to good effect, and Sharon reminded me of my senior high English teacher, Mrs. Deutsch, a tall and stern but kindly woman whose insights into literature went far beyond anything we could comprehend.

Poems about cats, envelopes of time, shit, a yellow tea cup, an uncooperative alarm clock. It was a good mix. We ran into Mike Hazard and his wife, Tressa, on the street before the reading and had a pleasant chat.

I get the impression that most of the people who attend these events know the artists on stage as friends, teachers, fellow-travelers, but that's not a bad thing. Rather, it's a community get-together, made more interesting by the fact that the specific attendees who show up differ from event to event. To me, the important thing is to hear the words given a face and a voice, embodied in a delivery. New Critics be damned, the tone of the accompanying banter also adds to the effect.

When we got home from the event, I took Mike Hazard's recent book, *The World Is Not Altogether Bad*, and read a few poems to Hilary while she chopped some onions for the frozen pizza we were about to slip into the oven.

Thanksgiving Reflections

I was sitting in the waiting room at a clinic the other day
thumbing through *The Seventeenth Century Background* by
Basil Willey when I came upon this appraisal of Sir Thomas
Browne (1605-1682):

> *Perhaps no writer is more truly representative of the dou-
> ble-faced age in which he lived, an age half scientific and
> half magical, half sceptical and half credulous, looking back
> in one direction to Maundeville, and forward to Newton.
> At one moment a Baconian experimentalist and herald of
> the new world, at another Browne is discoursing of cocka-
> trices and unicorns and mermaids in a tone which implies
> that though part of him is incredulous, the world is still
> incalculable enough to contain such marvels.*

We still live in that world of marvels, I think. We don't
know half as much as we think we know.

Willey adds:

> *At one moment [Browne] professes himself a follower of
> Hermes Trismegistus, and feels, pantheistically, "the warm
> gale and gentle ventilation" of the world-soul; at another,
> he accounts the world "not an Inn, but an Hospital; a place
> not to live, but to Dye in". He exhorts us now to "live by
> old Ethicks, and the classical rules of Honesty", and now to
> "Look beyond Antoninus, and terminate not thy morals in*

Seneca or Epictetus. Be a moralist of the Mount, and Chris-
tianize thy Notions." He had, in fact, what Mr. T. S. Eliot
has called the "unified sensibility" of the "metaphysicals,"
which was the offspring—perhaps unreproducible in differ-
ent circumstances—of a scholastic training blended with the
expansive curiosity of the Renaissance. It meant the capac-
ity to live in divided and distinguished worlds, and to pass
freely to and fro between one and another, to be capable of
many and varied responses to experience, instead of being
confined to a few stereotyped ones.

For a modern reader like me, the big problem with Sir
Thomas Browne is that he couldn't spell!

But leaving that issue aside, I think it's worth considering
how, if we care to, we can still live in an intellectual world as
rich as the one Browne inhabited, and why we should make
an effort to do so.

Anyone with an ounce or two of curiosity is likely to be
fascinated by the picture of the universe given to us by biologists, physicists, chemists, and other researchers of that ilk.
On the other hand, the philosophical community had failed
us big time by neglecting to emphasize how many questions
lie beyond the range of scientific research, and how much our
understanding of life and of ourselves depends on other dis-
ciplines—not only philosophy itself but also poetry, history,
and religion.

Our lack of clarity regarding the power and appeal of
these disparate but related spheres of thought—and the dif-
fering types of experience that feed them—makes it difficult
to properly emphasize the value and the limitations of any of
them.

A case in point: just this morning, after a first-of-the-season ski around Theodore Wirth Park, I was reading a review by Nicholas Kristof of Karen Armstrong's new book, *The Lost Art of Scripture*. Though I haven't read the book, a few days ago I listened to Kerry Miller interviewing Armstrong on the radio, so I already had some idea of what it's about, and Kristov's review underscored the same points.

In brief, Armstrong is arguing that scripture—Christian, Hindu, Confucian, or whatever—presents a vision of life in a different way than does the scientific community, and that "we" have lost the ability to receive its message. She goes on to suggest that an important part of that message lies beyond its factual or didactic content; it can be found in its sound, presentation, and embodiment.

Armstrong reminds us of how easy it can be to ridicule the nonsensical and contradictory aspects of scripture, and also to make use of it to defend bigoted attitudes and violent acts. But she also holds that looking for an accurate and all-encompassing representation of life from scripture misunderstands how those writings are designed to work. True once again, though she seems to be edging toward a "performative" interpretation of scripture rather than a narrative or metaphysical one. Kristov paraphrases :

> *It's like complaining about Shakespeare bending history, or protesting that a great song isn't factual ... Anyone who has been to a Catholic Mass or a Pentecostal service, or experienced the recitation of the Quran or a Tibetan Buddhist chant, knows that they couldn't fully be captured by a transcript any more than a song can be by its lyrics. I still don't understand Don McLean's classic song "American Pie," but it moves me every time I hear it. Music doesn't need to be factually accurate to be true.*

To which the rejoiner might be, "Yes, a piece of music or a theatrical production often moves us when it's beautiful, but that doesn't make it true, strictly speaking. The categories of experience are getting confused here, and need to be straightened out."

The other day I requested a copy of Durufle's Requiem from the library, and yesterday Hilary and I sat by the fire and listened to it. She was knitting; I was doing nothing. We enjoyed it so much we listened to it again, though it's in Latin and we had no idea what was being said beyond a few *Kyries* and *Agnus Deis*.

We were moved. Does that make us Christians? Probably not.

It's easy enough to hive off and discard those elements of scripture that expound an antiquated view of the physical cosmos, and it's also easy to cultivate an appreciation of the beauty of a given liturgy, without pondering the ethical and eschatological pronouncements that lie at the core of the faith in any great detail. Music and liturgy can bolster and strengthen a "faith," but it seems to me that faith must still be rooted in some form of understanding. If not, then it would be difficult to distinguish a religious faith from a social club or a choir group.

Then again, would it be too far off the mark to suggest that a religion *is* a social club, albeit of a special kind, created to facilitate and minister to its members' most important passages: birth, christening, communion, repentance, marriage, and death?

My parents dragged me and my brother to church for many years. They both sat up front in the chancel because they sang in the choir, and they had no idea what we were doing during the service. Nor did they care. They were shrewd enough to anticipate that some aspects of this beautiful world, full of reverence and holiness, might rub off on us no matter where we sat. We often played scissors-paper-rock up in the balcony, though sometimes we ran around in the basement. Occasionally we actually attended to the service—the readings, the psalms, the intercessions, and all the rest.

And some of it did rub off.

I actually found some of the sermons interesting. The minister, an East Coast transplant named Greenley, looked like a white-haired Efrim Zimbalist, Jr., the spitting image of an Old Testament patriarch. From the pulpit he analyzed Greek words and explained what the "fear" of God actually consisted of. His black Studebaker Lark convertible was always parked in front of the side door through which we usually entered the church on our way to the choir room.

Greenley's assistant was a tall, lanky recovering alcoholic named Andy. He typically wore a long black robe and had a disheveled Whitmanesque beard which gave him the look of a maladroit prophet who'd just returned from a few weeks in the desert. My mom found Greenley to be a little stuffy, I think, but she and Andy hit it off from the first. They were both interested in antique furniture. I think the desk sitting against the wall here in my office once belonged to him.

I don't remember much about the Sunday morning liturgy, but all lapsed Episcopalians probably remember these lines from the General Confession by heart.

We have done those things which we ought not to have done,
and we have not done those thing which we ought to have done,
and there is no health in us ...

At that age, my recurrent misdeeds were on the order of putting tin cans in the trash bag rather than the garbage bag.

I was also adept at forgetting to take the trash bag down to the basement to burn it in the incinerator, even after having been entreated to do so several times.

Yet even at an early age, the statement "there is no health in us" struck me as a bit extreme. Give me a break! No health whatsoever? Isn't that laying it on a little thick?

I also found the repeated reference during the readings to Israelites, Canaanites, Philistines and Maccabees incomprehensible and tedious.

But I digress. The point I'm trying to make (and so, I think, is Karen Armstrong) is that the sensations associated with a particular faith experience, repeated again and again, continue to resonate subliminally and eventually become a source of comfort (or nightmares, I suppose) long after we've rejected most of the theological particulars involved. I'm grateful to have been raised in a rich Anglican tradition in which the concept of sin tended to get slighted or ignored, and this gratitude extends beyond the aesthetics of choral harmonies and stained glass windows to the kind of ingrained and unthinking reverence that lends so much power to church events.

Perhaps one value Armstrong finds in orally transmitted scripture—a value she fears we're in danger of losing—is precisely this ritualistic liturgical repetition, which played a much larger role in daily life during ancient and medieval times, when many people couldn't read, than it does today.

But I think another aspect of scripture is also due for a revival: the poetry itself. And while we're at it, why not extend that interest more widely to encompass poetic works that do not claim for themselves the imprimatur of divine revelation. I'm not talking simply about verse here, but about all types of imaginative literature. Such creations summon experiences and types of understanding that can be had by no other means.

In his description of Browne's mental tool kit, cited above, Willey hits upon precisely the frame of mind needed to draw sustenance from that zone of experience and expression:

> *It meant the capacity to live in divided and distinguished worlds, and to pass freely to and fro between one and another, to be capable of many and varied responses to experience, instead of being confined to a few stereotyped ones.*

Here, in a typical passage, filled with Browne's halting yet elegant delivery and terrible orthography, he draws upon his medical background to consider where in the body the soul resides—he can't seem to find the relevant organ.

> *In our study of Anatomy there is a masse of mysterious Philosophy, and such as reduced the very Heathens to Divinitie; yet amongst all those rare discoveries, and curious pieces I finde in the fabricke of man, I doe not so much content my selfe as in that I finde not, that is, no Organ or instrument for the rationall soule; for in the braine, which we tearme the seate of reason, there is not any thing of moment more than I can discover in the cranie of a beast: and this is a sensible and no inconsiderable argument of the inorganity of the soule, at least in that sense we usually so receive it. Thus are we men, and we know not how; there is something in us, that can be without us, and will be after us, though it is strange that it hath no history, what it was before us, nor can tell how it entered in us.*

Browne goes on to consider what the human body is actually made of:

Now for the walls of flesh, wherein the soule doth seeme to be immured before the Resurrection, it is nothing but an elementall composition, and a fabricke that must fall to ashes; All flesh is grasse, is not onely metaphorically, but literally true, for all those creatures which we behold, are but the hearbs of the field, digested into flesh in them, or more remotely carnified in our selves. Nay further, we are what we all abhorre, Antropophagi and Cannibals, devourers not onely of men, but of our selves; and that not in an allegory, but a positive truth; for all this masse of flesh which wee behold, came in at our mouths: this frame wee looke upon, hath beene upon our trenchers; In briefe, we have devoured our selves and yet do live and remaine our selves.

Now there's some food for post-Thanksgiving thought.

Love of Leeks

I sometimes rise before six, make the coffee (grinding the beans as quietly as a Krups electric coffee-grinder allows) and sit in the Poang chair by the front window watching light come into the sky. A few mornings ago, as I sat at my predawn post, the word "strata" came to mind. Why? Rummaging through my grab bag of associations, I quickly rejected the opera singer Teresa Stratas and the Fellini film *La Strada* from consideration.

When the word "stirato" drifted into view I knew I was getting warm. Stirato bread, as you probably know, is like an Italian baguette, and there was a glass container of bread, sliced into small cubes, sitting on the kitchen counter. I'd seen it there while making the coffee.

But the word "strata," I seemed to recall, referred to a breakfast dish consisting mostly of bread and cheese. Should I make some such thing?

These idle thoughts stood to attention when it occurred to me that there was a leek lying on the bottom shelf of the refrigerator. A leek strata! Such a thing might not exist, but it was suddenly clear I had to make one.

It didn't take long to find a long string of recipes for strata online. I chose one from a website called Pioneer Woman—because it offered four or five variations and made the process of assembly otherwise very casual. I converted the text to a Word document and printed it out.

Five eggs, two cups of milk, four cups of hand-torn day-old bread, some cheese, and whatever else you have available. The recipe called for eight strips of bacon and a third of a cup of shallots. I made do with my single precious leek, which I sliced lengthwise down the middle as quietly as I could, and then into quarters in the same direction, finally cutting it crossways into ¼ inch pieces. I sautéed the little pieces in butter for a while and also got a bag of parsley out of the freezer and tossed a generous handful of surprisingly green and aromatic leaves into the mix.

Next, I fetched two stubby pieces of hard white cheese from the cheese drawer, both with rind attached. One was Gruyere, I'm pretty sure. The other, who knows? A dash of salt, a big dash of dry mustard, then into a lightly greased 8 x 8-inch pan. You're supposed to let it chill in the refrigerator for six hours, but that wasn't going to happen. I slipped it into the oven at 350 degrees to bake for 50 minutes. A few minutes later, when Hilary came around the corner, a variety of pleasant aromas were emanating from the kitchen.

The results (if I do say so myself) were outstanding, and the effect was heightened by the spontaneous nature of the event. The day-old bread (actually three days old) was from Rustica, the city's premier bakery, which helped, but it was the subtle elegance of the leek, I think, that put the dish over the top.

Can a vegetable be elegant? I hope you know what I mean. Yes, a leek is just a glorified onion, but I have long since grown suspicious of this usage of the word "just." Most of the good things in life are "just" better versions of the crummy things in life.

It's true that leeks cost more than onions, but a single leek from Trader Joe's costs no more than a fancy apple or vine-ripened tomato. So what? And at mid-summer farmers markets you can get a bundle of three long, tender stalks for $2.

It's been said that eating leeks will keep your hair from turning gray. I have not found that to be true.

Leeks have been held in high regard since ancient times. They appear in Egyptian tomb hieroglyphics and figure prominently in Apicius's famous Roman cookbook. Yet no one has been able to put their unique flavor into words precisely. Waverly Root describes them as "less fine but more robust than asparagus," a remark that seems very odd to me. The *Oxford Companion to Food* refers to their "mild, sweet flavor."

Off the top of my head, I'd say they taste like ethereal onions infused with a hint of thyme. But words aren't worth much in a situation like this. You just have to try them.

Ortega – Lao Tzu

C ombing the shelves in the bedroom a few days ago in the spirit of social distancing, I happened upon a row of well-worn orange paperbacks published by W. W. Norton, all of them bearing the name of the Spanish philosopher José Ortega y Gasset on the spine.

No one reads Ortega nowadays—at least no one that I know. And the titles, most of which appeared between the two world wars, have an old-fashioned and slightly generic ring: *Man and People, Man and Crisis, The Modern Theme, The Dehumanization of Art, History as a System*. Ortega wrote his most famous work, *The Revolt of the Masses*, in 1914.

Considered all in all, these titles conjure a point of view galaxies removed from the issues and perspectives that excite young people and academics today. What they fail to suggest is how wide-ranging Ortega's interests were and how comfortable he was raising basic metaphysical issues without feeling the need to explore every possible objection that we might present or puff up his thoughts with obscure terminology. Ortega often referred to philosophy as a form of noble sport, and his writings almost invariably carry a jaunty, even journalistic flair.

I ended up reading a short essay from the collection *Concord and Liberty.* It carries the ambitious title "Notes on Thinking—Its Creation of the World and Its Creation of God."

According to Ortega, much of Western philosophy, building on the Greek notion of "aletheia," the discovery of hidden being, concerns itself with establishing connections between our thoughts and the things "out there." We take that to be "thinking."

But in his view, this orientation isn't a necessity. Rather, it's a choice we make about the relative importance of things. Other people, other cultures, have made different choices.

As a young man Ortega studied for quite a while in Marburg, Germany, which was then the capital of neo-Kantianism. This led him on to considerations of Edmund Husserl, who explored perhaps the most attenuated version of that approach. Husserl's phenomenological method was an attempt to make an end run past the problems of verification posed by the empirical approach. It focused not on how we experience things, but on how we experience *our experiences* of things. By solipsistically avoiding the challenges and vagaries of the world "out there" Husserl and his students felt they had somehow purified their inquiry. Ortega may have been trained in this discipline, but by the time he wrote "Notes on Thinking," he'd long since outgrown it.

> *The sphere of absolute reality—Husserl's* reine Erlebnisse *(pure experiences)—has, in spite of its juicy name, nothing to do with life; it is, strictly speaking, the opposite of life.*

Ortega eventually brings us around to the point that the "ground" of belief upon which individuals build their thoughts differs at different times and places, and therefore, their notions of what truth looks like will also differ. He points to the Buddhists by way of example. Their basic belief in the immortality of the ego, doomed to live an endless succession of lives, shapes their ideas about life and behavior.

The Hebrews, on the other hand, believe in the indomitable will of God, out of which everything flows. That being the case, for them no purpose is served in investigating the static "being" of particular things. To a Jew the Greek concept of "aletheia," the discovery of hidden being, is entirely beside the point. What interests him or her is "emunah," the Hebrew word for truth, which is rooted in the future, and also in the notion of firmness—the truth, the firmness, of God's will. *Amen. So shall it be.*

In a footnote Ortega observes that Aristotle, in his effort to describe what the "substance" of a thing is, finds it necessary to concoct an entire sentence by way of naming it: "a-thing-being-what-it-was." Though a being is what it is *now*, Aristotle's definition refers to its durability through time.

In the space of a few pages Ortega has given us a good deal to think about. Especially the importance of time. Whether the connections he draws between the static, thing-oriented philosophy of Greece and the general aridity of modern thought are valid I couldn't say, but he was not alone in working to establish a more dynamic approach to describing thought and its purposes, as a means to get a handle on "life itself." Over the course of a long career as one of Europe's most eminent philosophers he employed several concepts in turn—vital reason, trajectory, perspectivism, historical reason—to explain how thinking works and what it's for, though he developed none of these concepts to the extent that it became philosophical common coin. (Then again, philosophers are seldom interested in dealing in their colleagues' currency, especially if it's in Spanish. They'd rather mint their own.)

To my ear, most of what Ortega has to say here is true, but I found the most interesting points to follow from his acknowledgment that there is more than one set of assumptions available to us as we work to construct a coherent picture of our place in the world. He mentions the Buddhists, the Hebrews, the Greeks.

A few days after reading this essay, I ran across a book on the For Sale book cart in the lobby of my local library, *Dao De Jing: a Philosophical Translation*. I had checked this book out years ago, but never got a chance to take a serious look at it.

I bought it, and, struggling under the burden of a tenacious cold, I read the introduction. Brilliant! Here, I said to myself, is a description of life and an approach to experience that Ortega would have approved in every detail. First and foremost among its underlying beliefs or parameters is the rejection of the idea of "being." Second is the understanding that self and circumstances are inextricably intertwined. (Ortega: "I am myself and my circumstances.")

There is eloquence in the prose of Roger Ames and David Hall, the translators who wrote the introduction, as they attempt to convey the unique qualities of the Chinese manuscript without falling into the many traps that common language usage in Western tongues present. Here is a typical passage, which might have been lifted directly out of one of Ortega's essays:

> *What encourages us within a Western metaphysical tradition to separate time and space is our inclination, inherited from the Greeks, to see things in the world as fixed in their*

formal aspect, and thus as bounded and limited. If instead of giving ontological privilege to the formal aspect of phenomena, we were to regard them as having parity in their formal and changing aspects, we might be more like classical China in temporalizing them in light of their ceaseless transformation, and conceive of them more as "events" than as "things." In this processual worldview, each phenomenon is some unique current or impulse within a temporal flow.

But Ames and Hall have an advantage over Ortega. He's trying to wrench a long-standing tradition from its path, while remaining within it. They're merely saying, "Hey, take a look at this entirely different way of approaching life and experience." They're referring, of course, to the text of the *Dao De Jing,* also known as the *Lao Tzu* or the *I Ching.*

As for their translation itself, it strikes me as more meaningful than the standard one—if there is a standard one—but also wordier and less "poetic."

A second set of philosophical assumptions also came to mind as I read Ortega's essay: those of Hegel. Hegel is well-known for having remarked, "Nothing can be predicated of Being." He replaced that concept with the concept of Spirit, and a *restless* spirit at that, developing dialectically through time. The "things" that may interest us he construes as "objective spirit." That is to say, they're concrete deposits—institutions, works of art, historical narratives, feats of engineering—that reflect the condition of spirit at that time and nourish its further development. They are to be admired and utilized but also to be risen above as new circumstances call for new creations and iterations.

Why Hegel felt the need to attach the word "absolute" to spirit is beyond me, but he did. That was a big mistake.

After finishing Ortega's little essay, I was inspired to pull another book off the shelf: *The Imperative of Modernity: an Intellectual Biography of José Ortega de Gasset* by Rockwell Gray. It's a brilliant and eloquent volume. One of the passages that really hit home, during my random perusal, compared Ortega to the French *philosophes* of the eighteenth century.

> *Although much of the thematic content of Ortega's mature philosophical work came from outside Spain and must be seen within the larger history of European neo-Kantianism, phenomenology, and existentialism, his early work and his lifelong concern for the condition of Spain cannot be understood without reference to major Spanish reformists of the later nineteenth century.*

Gray adds that

> *the original model for the essay of social criticism came into Spain from the French Enlightenment and the philosophes.* [They] *provided the more distant historical precedent for the kind of far-ranging essay writing that Ortega was ultimately to refine in his modern Spanish prose. It is also among* [them] *that we find an early source of modern historicist philosophy—the assertion that man lives in time with no guarantee of a beginning or a destiny beyond this world ... In this broader view, it is possible to consider Ortega a latter-day* philosophe *despite his very considerable indebtedness to various German thinkers of the late nineteenth and early twentieth centuries.*

A very good point, with respect not only to Ortega's choice of themes, but also to his cheery and accessible style. Diderot and Ortega, for example, would make a good College Bowl team.

But during these strange and difficult times, perhaps the

Dao has something less intellectual but more appropriate to offer us. I just now opened the translation of Hall and Ames to verse eleven.

Extend your utmost emptiness as far as you can
And do your best to preserve your equilibrium.

Now as for equilibrium—this is called returning to the
propensity of things,
And returning to the propensity of things is common sense.

Using common sense is acuity,
While failing to use it is to lose control.

And to try to do anything while out of control is to court
disaster.

Darkness and
Music and Lights

The absence of snow has made the season seem darker. We got a little dusting on Monday night—just enough to remind us of what we're missing. The next morning there were raccoon tracks all over the street, running from one curb-side drainage grate to another. They also proceeded around our garage and up onto the back deck. I didn't need to check if there was any feed left in the feeders. Not a chance.

Out on the road there were also a few deer tracks, one squirrel, and perhaps a cat.

Evenings have been brightened by music. A Messiah sing-a-long which was plenty rousing, though slightly less compelling at Orchestra Hall than the one we attended a few years ago at Central Lutheran Church downtown. An Anglican ceremony of lessons and carols at St. Mark's Episcopal Cathedral. These are the familiar readings, the familiar hymns, along with some beautiful renderings of unfamiliar carols sung by a very polished choir. And how convenient that we could participate on a Sunday evening at five, rather than struggling to stay awake on Christmas Eve.

The most unusual concert we heard was given by the Rose Ensemble, who performed a selection of Christmas pieces written during the seventeenth century for the cathedral church on the island of Malta. None of the pieces were familiar, which isn't surprising, considering the scores have been languishing in some archive on a Mediterranean island for the last three hundred years. And the lyrics to the pieces were in Latin, with one or two exceptions, so the event had very little of a Christmas "feel" to it. Yet the concert was gorgeous, due to both the quality of the voices and the richness of the harmonies involved, which struck me—unschooled in the period though I am—as less flamboyant that the music of Monteverdi, more concerned with texture, less with ornamentation and vocal display.

On the longest night of the year, we were visited by two great lights. The lesser of these was the fire I built in the fire pit out on the deck. The greater was the arrival of our friend Dave, who visits us annually at about this time of year. Dave and I have been friends since high school, and Hilary has known him almost as long. He moved to Texas maybe forty years ago, but he still has family in Minnesota, and we've kept in touch.

Over the years we've followed Dave's career in the world of art handling and installation. It got more complicated about ten years ago when he and a few colleagues decided to start their own business. At about the same time, Dave bought a cinder-block warehouse in a run-down neighborhood near the Trinity River. The living quarters he installed left plenty of room for storing the vast collection of mission furniture he'd accumulated over the years at small-town shops and auctions. Dave was also convinced that when the city finally built a bridge across the river, his property would end up being worth a lot more than he'd paid for it.

A decade later, Dave's business is thriving, the bridge has

been built, and development is well underway all around him. But the city of Dallas has been putting the squeeze on him, granting an easement to widen the road in front of his building, threatening to condemn the property—doing everything in its power, in short, to remove him without pay him a fair market price for his home and warehouse.

Dave fought city hall, and he lost. But during the process, the developers finally realized that they were also losing vast sums waiting for Dave's endgame with the city to play itself out, and they made him an offer. It wasn't what the property would have gone for on the market, but it was enough for Dave to buy 78 acres of land in the country south of Dallas, complete with living quarters, warehouse, pond, woodlot, creek, and plenty of buzzards, coyotes, and feral hogs.

Meanwhile, he's been gradually stepping back from the business he started and is now in the process of selling his shares. Dave will soon be a gentleman farmer. "What do you mean? I *am* a gentleman farmer!" he says. And he's already got plans for building a bridge across the creek, buying a tractor and some goats, and sitting out on the front porch in the evenings, watching the sun go down and listening to the whippoorwills.

It's a far cry from the hype and worry of the Texas art world, and not a life-style Dave was thinking much about a few years ago. But he's taken risks and made bold decisions before. There's been dissonance in his life from time to time, but hearing about these new developments around the firepit on the deck, it sounded to me less like a false cadence than a grand resolution, rich in elements to be whipped up into an entirely new movement.

First Snowfall

It does something to the heart—deflates it, I think, and sends it scurrying for shelter. But it isn't an altogether bad feeling. There's an element of relief involved, and also one of surrender. At the same time, one feels a secret and almost conspiratorial joy. Now we can start thinking about "inner" things, sit in front of the fire at 5 p.m. while the cauliflower for the spaghetti sauce roasts in the oven.

With whom are we conspiring? With the night, of course. And with that inner flame that begins to reassert itself as the abundant heat of summer dwindles.

When the snow started to fall, I was sitting in a café with my father-in-law, Gene, who's ninety-two. He said, "When the Armistice Day Blizzard hit, I was in the bar of the Lemington Hotel with two friends. We were trapped there for three days."

I had never heard that story before.

Gene and I had just attended a morning concert together. Three of the four composers involved—Smit, Schulhoff, and Karel—died in concentration camps. The lobby of the church where the performance took place contained an exhibit of brightly color photographs taken recently of men and women, all residents of the Twin Cities, who had survived those camps and are presumably still alive.

The music being performed was full of festive French carnival colors in the manner of Poulenc, Milhaud, and Auric, and sprightly Czech folk dance tunes, somewhat rearranged and homogenized for the concert stage—though they kept the 5/4 time. I liked them all.

At the end of World War II, Gene was among the GIs who came upon and liberated the concentration camps. No one told those young men what to expect. No one told them the camps were there.

I have heard that story before. Gene didn't feel the need to bring it up again.

No, we talked about the son-in-law of a family friend, a seasoned chef who had catered the Ryder's Cup and was then invited to do the same for Prince's funeral. We talked about the historian Joseph Ellis and the travel writer Norman Lewis. We talked about nieces and nephews, jazz singers and retirement homes.

The concert hall had been filled with elderly women and men who sometimes had trouble making their way across the lobby, but who were nevertheless continuing to find ways to enjoy life. And here we were, as the snow flashed by the window in violent streaks and began to obscure the still-green grass, chowing down as if there were no tomorrow.